Francis Charles Montague

Arnold Toynbee

Seventh Series

Francis Charles Montague

Arnold Toynbee
Seventh Series

ISBN/EAN: 9783337141042

Printed in Europe, USA, Canada, Australia, Japan

Cover: Foto ©ninafisch / pixelio.de

More available books at **www.hansebooks.com**

I

ARNOLD TOYNBEE

ARNOLD TOYNBEE

1852-1883

JOHNS HOPKINS UNIVERSITY STUDIES
IN
HISTORICAL AND POLITICAL SCIENCE

HERBERT B. ADAMS, Editor

History is past Politics and Politics present History—*Freeman*

SEVENTH SERIES

I

ARNOLD TOYNBEE

BY F. C. MONTAGUE
Fellow of Oriel College, Oxford

WITH AN ACCOUNT OF THE WORK OF TOYNBEE HALL IN EAST LONDON,
BY PHILIP LYTTELTON GELL, M. A., CHAIRMAN OF THE COUNCIL.
ALSO AN ACCOUNT OF THE NEIGHBORHOOD GUILD IN
NEW YORK, BY CHARLES B. STOVER, A. B.

PUBLICATION AGENCY OF THE JOHNS HOPKINS UNIVERSITY
JANUARY, 1889

ARNOLD TOYNBEE.

I.

Arnold **Toynbee**, the second son of Joseph Toynbee, **the** distinguished **aurist**, was born on the 23rd **of** August, 1852, in Savile Row, London. Whilst he was **yet an** infant, **his** family removed to a house at Wimbledon in **Surrey**, where he spent the greater part of his childhood. **Mr.** Toynbee is remembered by friends to have taken the **keenest interest in** Arnold of whom, when only four years old, he spoke **as his** child of promise, and on whose development he exercised **a** very powerful influence. He was always anxious to **improve** the condition of the poor, and assisted in the erection of model cottages and the establishment of a lecture hall at Wimbledon. He employed Arnold whilst yet very young in the lectures upon elementary science which he used to give to the working-men of the neighborhood. Nor was it only by setting **an** example of public spirit that Mr. Toynbee did **much to form** the character **of his son.** He was a lover of **art, a discerning** collector of pictures, who knew how to communicate to others his enthusiasm for the works of great masters, and like all who sincerely love art, he took an especial delight in natural beauty. Wimbledon was then a pretty village situated in a fresh rural landscape, the fairest to be found in the immediate vicinity of **London.** In later years Arnold Toynbee would look back as to the **happiest** hours of **childhood** to those rambles **over** **Wimbledon Common on which** his father would take out a **volume of poetry and as they** rested in **pleasant** spots here and there **read** aloud such passages as a child could feel at least, if not understand.

Whilst yet very young Arnold Toynbee delighted in reading history, especially military history, and his favorite pastime was to construct mimic fortifications, which he built with more than childish precision and armed with the heaviest ordnance procurable. Always delicate and exquisitely sensitive to pain, he had not the animal courage common to strong, healthy boys; yet, by the unanimous testimony of brothers and of schoolfellows, he was singularly fearless, throwing himself into everything which he attempted with an impetuosity which made him forgetful of consequences and even of actual suffering. With this high-strung vehemence he united a very resolute will. From first to last, he was one of those who would sooner be dashed to pieces than fail to climb any height which they have once determined to surmount. In later life these qualities were tempered by scrupulous anxiety to be just and fair, by a beautiful kindliness and delicacy; but in early youth they were accompanied with a violent temper, and an excess of self-confidence. He was but eight years old when he went to his first school, a private establishment at Blackheath, where he became the leader in amusement and mischief of boys much older than himself. Having once planned with many of his schoolfellows a joke to be executed when the master's back was turned, he failed to notice the entrance by an opposite door of another master and the hasty retreat of all his accomplices who left him alone in the middle of the floor, absorbed in the execution of a caricature for which he alone suffered, although all were guilty.

As a schoolboy and ever after he was slow in acquiring a knowledge of any subject distasteful to him, such as languages or mathematics, but showed great power in grasping any subject which, like history, fired his imagination. Rapidity of acquisition was never the distinguishing quality of his intelligence. A fastidious taste and eager passion for truth made half knowledge distasteful to him; and whole knowledge comes readily to no man. At school he grew so decided in his preference for a military life that, when he was fourteen years of age, his father sent him to a college which prepared candidates for army examinations. Here he held his own among comrades who were not very congenial. He had a boy's instinct for games and his swiftness of foot and high spirit made him an excellent football player; but he played football, as he did everything else, with an eagerness which overstrained his delicate nervous system, and in consequence he suffered from illness and sleepless nights. Here too he enlarged his reading in history and surprised his tutors by the force and originality of his essays. He began to feel an impulse towards purely intellectual pursuits and an unfitness for the career of a soldier. His father was no longer living, and, at his own request, he left the college when he was about sixteen years of age. He had not made many friends among his fellow students, but he had impressed the masters as a youth of singular talent and singular elevation of character; so much so, that one of them, making him a present on his departure, asked him to accept it as a token " of real respect and esteem."

Having abandoned all thoughts of entering the army, Toynbee next thought of preparing himself to enter the Civil Service; and with this view spent the two following years in reading at home and in attending lectures at King's College, London. Subsequently he resolved to be called to the Bar; a resolution which he only abandoned after a painful struggle and in obedience to circumstances. These were to him years of painful uncertainty. Although he had many who were very dear to him, none fully understood, certainly he did not himself understand the tendency of that inward restlessness which he seems to have experienced at this period. It is the fashion to say that youth is the happiest season of life, and, in one sense, this is true, but in another sense it is equally true, that the youth of thoughtful persons is often racked with pains which they cannot express and which are

not the less real, because their elders can prescribe nothing
better than platitudes. The sufferings of middle and of latter
life bear no more analogy to these pains than does the anguish
of a toothache to the torture of cutting one's teeth. Whilst
the surface-current of Toynbee's mind set now towards this,
now towards that profession, the undercurrent set more and
more steadily towards the pursuit of truth. At length that
current swept him right away and he deliberately resolved to
devote his life to the study of history and of the philosophy
of history. In order to secure quiet for his meditations,
Toynbee took lodgings, first, in the village of Bracknell in
Berks, and afterwards in the village of East Lulworth on the
Dorsetshire coast; in these retreats he spent many months.
For the first time he began to see what he really wished
to do, and, still more important, what it was that he really
could do.

Toynbee's aspirations and plans of study of this period may
best be gathered from a letter which he wrote to the late Mr.
Hinton, a warm friend of his father and a spirit in many
ways congenial to his own. It will be necessary to refer
hereafter to the correspondence in which this letter occurs.
It is dated the 18th of September, 1871, when the writer had
just completed his nineteenth year and was written from East
Lulworth. The passage relevant in this context is as follows :—

"For myself, I have, since the beginning of April, with
the exception of a short interval in July, been reading alone
at this quiet little village near the seacoast, ostensibly with a
view to a University career; but determined to devote my
life and such power as I possess to the study of the philosophy
of history. With this object in view, I have no inclination to
enter any profession; nor do I think it probable that I shall
compete for a scholarship at the University. To these pursuits I wish to give my whole life. The small means at my
disposal, and those which without the expenditure of much
time I hope to be able to add to them, will be sufficient for

my maintenance. I do not care to spend my life in acquiring material benefits which might have an evil, and at any rate could not have a good effect upon me. These ideas may appear ridiculous in one so young and of powers so immature, but they are not the result of mere ambition, or of an empty desire for fame in itself, or for the rewards with which it is accompanied. My sole, and so far as it can be so, unalloyed motive is the pursuit of truth ; and for truth I feel I would willingly sacrifice prospects of the most dazzling renown. I do not even think myself capable of accomplishing any work of importance. If my labors merely serve to assist another in the great cause, I shall be satisfied."

As time went on Toynbee found reason to vary the programme of work laid down in this letter, but he never swerved from the spirit expressed therein. Few men have combined so much self-confidence with so much modesty, or have been so entirely absorbed in their work, so totally free from motives of vanity or of egotism. Yet a solitary life was neither natural nor wholesome for one so young. At this time he was an absolute recluse in his habits, and even when at home shut himself up with his books, disdaining, like so many clever boys, to mix with ordinary society. Happily, this stage of his life was not to continue much longer. When he had reached the age of twenty-one years, he found himself master of a small capital, and trusting to this for maintenance during a university career, he became a member of Pembroke College, Oxford, in the January of 1873. In the autumn of that year he resolved to compete for a scholarship in Modern History at Balliol College. Here he was unsuccessful. He had brought up to the University a considerable knowledge of history and of general literature. But he had accumulated knowledge in order to satisfy his own cravings, not the curiosity of examiners. He had accumulated it without advice or assistance, and had never gone through that singular process whereby a lad who knows little and cares nothing for knowledge is enabled to turn out dozens of tolerably correct essays upon dozens of great subjects. In short, he had not read for examination, and, when examined, could not do himself justice.

From this repulse, however, Toynbee derived a benefit impossible to estimate too highly. As he had read and reflected by himself, and had honestly worked out his own opinions, he imagined himself to have gone deeper and further than was really the case. Extreme, therefore, was his disgust when one of his examiners, in explaining to him the reasons of his ill-success, said: " You have picked up your ideas from hearing the clever talk of London society, and you have written your papers just as you would talk." He used afterwards to say that this criticism, baseless as it was, had done him the greatest good imaginable. It is true that the incisive way of putting ideas which struck his examiners derived itself from an incisive way of thinking, and continued with him throughout life. But it is also true that, in the present stage of learning, the student who does not avail himself of the recognized methods is like a traveller who prefers his own legs to an express train. With all their faults, the universities supply to the scholar that which he cannot dispense with and cannot get so well anywhere else—the methods elaborated by thousands of his predecessors; the correction supplied by contemporaries equal or superior to himself; the powerful current of spiritual electricity set up in the assemblage of so many eager wits. Had Toynbee never gone to the University, he might have remained all his life groping towards results long since attained by men far inferior in force of character and of intelligence. His new experience taught him his defects and how to amend them.

But the immediate result of the scholarship examination was one of those tedious illnesses which consumed so much of the short time allotted to him upon earth. He was forced to leave Oxford, to suspend all his work, to go down into the country and try slowly and painfully to rally his exhausted powers. From this and many other such intervals of mournful leisure he, indeed, drew profit, as such a nature draws profit from every experience. For his friends they were an unmixed sadness. It was not until a year had passed away that he was able to return to Oxford. In the January of 1875 he became a commoner of Balliol College. His real undergraduate life commences from this date; and here the narrative of his early years may best conclude.

II.

Toynbee's **health** continued to be so delicate that he could **not read for** honors in any school, much less compete for any university prizes or distinctions. As he was unable to study hard for more than an average of two or three **hours a day,** he was obliged to content himself with a pass degree. Yet few men have derived more profit from a university course. He continued to read widely and judiciously. The Master and the tutors of Balliol College fully comprehended his great gifts and great embarrassments, and gave him sympathy, guidance and frank, discerning criticism. He always gratefully acknowledged **much** he owed especially to the **Master and to** the late Professor Thomas Hill Green. As **regards his merely academic** studies, it is here enough to **say that he took a** pass degree in the summer of 1878.

Every **one** who knows Oxford will allow that, valuable as is the teaching supplied by **the** university and the colleges, it is hardly more valuable than the genial intercourse between the young inquisitive spirits there assembled.

Although Toynbee had hitherto lived in seclusion, he fell very readily into this intercourse and gave even more good than he received. He was in truth formed for society and friendship. **At** this time he was very comely and attractive in appearance. An oval **face,** a high forehead crowned with masses of soft brown hair, features very clearly cut, a straight nose **and** a rather large, full-lipped mouth, only needed more color to produce the impression of beauty; and even the color

wanting to his gray eyes and brown complexion was supplied
when he grew warm in conversation by a lighting up of his
whole countenance, a brilliant yet soft irradiation, which
charmed the beholder and can never be forgotten by those
who knew him well. Together with this winning countenance
he had a manner singularly frank, open and animated. A
student and an invalid, he was free from the vexatious oddities of either; was neither shy nor slow nor abstracted nor
languid, but always prompt and lively. He talked extremely
well, without exactly conversing. For that delightful pastime
which the French call a *causerie* he was not altogether adapted.
For that the mind must be habitually at ease—not unemployed,
but never taxed up to its utmost strength, not strained by
crowding ideas on vehement feelings. Toynbee, as time went
on, came to concentrate more and more upon a few momentous
subjects which were ever present to him, concerning which he
spoke with wonderful eloquence and enthusiasm. The faces
of listeners supplied him with the stimulus which his sensitive
temperament and weak body required. He never was quite
happy in writing out his thoughts. He complained that they
came upon his mind faster than he could set them down on
paper. That he had real literary talent, many passages in the
volume of fragments published after his death show; but
nothing which he has written gives any idea of his power of
expressing himself by word of mouth. Although he spoke
rapidly and copiously, he never was betrayed into a vulgar
phrase or slovenly construction; he spoke as one to whom
idiomatic utterance is natural, correctly and forcibly, without
the cant phrases of the undergraduate or the studied negli-
gence of the college tutor. Nor did he, like so many other
exuberant speakers, suggest to those who heard him that he
spoke out of a passion for display. If he talked much it was
because he forgot himself in his subject. No man ever was
more willing to hear all that others had to say, or sought with
more kind and courteous attention to encourage criticism, even
opposition. Naturally combative and fond of controversy, he

was never betrayed into those little breaches of amenity so common even among men of good temper and good breeding when heated by argument. Naturally somewhat intolerant, he had schooled himself into genuine tolerance. Naturally sensitive and excitable, he had, whilst retaining all his original warmth, subdued in a surprising degree the impulse to exaggerate. Everything he said bore the impress of an exquisitely fine nature. One could not listen to him without admiring, or argue against him without loving. One could no more say a brutal or profane thing to him than to the most delicate lady. Not that he was finical, or censorious, or assumed the right to check others in an impertinent or condescending tone, but that no man of good feeling could, without a cutting pang of remorse, shock such an exquisite sensibility.

Good looks, talent, information and social gifts are more than enough to gain friends at the University; but Toynbee had many other attractions. He was in all senses of the word, sympathetic. He had sympathy for men's sufferings, for their interests and pursuits, even for their failings and misdeeds. No matter what the troubles of an acquaintance—ill health, ill success, disappointment or poverty, they always seemed to raise his value in Toynbee's eyes. Nor was compassion with Toynbee a mere sentiment. He was always eager to assist in any useful way, studied his friend's affairs as if they were his own, gave the warmest, sincerest encouragement to the desponding, the kindest, tenderest criticism to the erring, yet seemed never to expect any thanks and to take gratitude as a free gift. Out of his small store of life and strength he bestowed freely upon all. With this evangelical charity he joined the widest sympathy of another kind. All fellow students were his brethren. Their labors, their acquisitions, their successes were his. He admired talent of all sorts, and rejoiced in all achievements which enriched the life of the individual or of the race.

For a man of this temperament the years spent at college are his happiest. The years that come after may bring the philosophic mind; but they cannot add the joy and **the fulness** of life. Toynbee had not hitherto felt how much he was alive; he felt it now, and was charmed with a new sense of expansion. "The garden quadrangle at Balliol," he writes to a friend, "is where one walks at night, and listens to the wind in the trees, and weaves the stars into the web of one's thoughts; where one gazes from the pale inhuman moon to the ruddy light of the windows, and hears broken notes of music and laughter and the complaining murmur of the railroad in the distance. . . . The life here is very sweet and full of joy; at Oxford, after **all**, one's ideal of happy life is nearer being realized than anywhere else—I **mean** the ideal **of** gentle, equable, intellectual intercourse, with something **of a** prophetic glow about it, glancing brightly into the future, yet always embalming itself in the memory **as** a resting-place for the **soul in** a future that may be dark and troubled after all, with **little in** it but disastrous failure."

Soon after Arnold Toynbee came **up to Oxford**, Mr. Ruskin, then Professor of Fine **Arts in the** University, made a characteristic endeavor to illustrate the dignity and good effects of even **the** coarsest bodily toil. He persuaded **many** undergraduates to work under him at the repair of **a** road **in** the village of Hinksey near Oxford. Among these undergraduates was Toynbee, who rose by his zeal to the rank of a foreman. He was thus entitled to appear frequently at those breakfasts which Mr. Ruskin gave to his young friends and enlivened with quaint, eloquent conversation. Upon men like Toynbee, intercourse with Mr. Ruskin had a stimulating effect more durable **than** the actual improvement of the road near Hinksey. Toynbee came to think very differently **from** Mr. Ruskin upon many subjects, and especially upon democracy; but always regarded him with reverence and affection. About the same time Toynbee joined **the** Oxford University Rifles, because he thought that every **man** should qualify himself to take part in the defence **of his** country; he was unable, however, long to fulfil the duties of **a** volunteer.

His bodily weakness, which also forbade him to study long or with strict regularity, constrained him, as it were, to enjoy Oxford and its society more than he might otherwise have allowed himself to do. It brought another indirect advantage of even more consequence. It saved him from the bad effects of our fashionable method of intellectual instruction, which tends to make the student read as much and as widely as possible without any reference to the effect which reading may have upon the mind. Toynbee was naturally exact in his intelligence, and gained in accuracy and thoroughness as time went on. He derived nothing but good from his studies as an undergraduate. Older than most undergraduates, he felt the genial influence of Oxford, without being overpowered by it. Without ceasing to be original he appropriated, more freely than he had ever done before, the ideas of his time. Soon after coming into residence at Balliol College, he had decided to take political economy for his province and to study it upon historical methods. Political economy attracted him chiefly as affording instruction respecting the conditions of social life, and his interest in that science was singularly intertwined with interest in other subjects, in popular prejudice the most remote from it of any.

Religion daily came to occupy his thoughts more and more. In his boyhood it had no very important place. He had received the usual instruction in religious subjects and this had, as usual, made very little impression. His father, although, full of religious feeling, had perhaps wisely abstained from indoctrinating his children with any rigid creed or drilling them in any strict forms of worship. When Arnold Toynbee had reached the age at which life first becomes serious, his first aspirations were, as we have seen, purely intellectual. He wished to live for others and resolved to live for them as a student. An increase of knowledge was the blessing which he wished to confer upon his race. But his early ideal was not to give him full satisfaction. Even at the age of nineteen years, as is shown by the correspondence with Mr. Hinton above quoted, he had begun to ponder the most vexing problems which offer themselves to the devout mind. The correspondence turned chiefly upon Mr. Hinton's book "The Mystery of Pain." Mr. Hinton's speculative enthusiasm, his real elevation of mind and sympathy with religious cravings were such as might well fascinate an eager clever lad arrived at the age when the very few who are not absorbed in careless gaiety are so frequently devoured by ascetic earnestness. As time went on the spell which Mr. Hinton exercised over Arnold Toynbee lost much of its force. The young man came to see that Mr. Hinton's remarkable book leaves the mystery as mysterious as it was before, and felt perhaps a growing sense of discord between his own nature and that of his early teacher. Their exchange of ideas nevertheless marked an epoch in Toynbee's life.

His religious development was not checked but accelerated by his residence at Oxford. "Most men," he said, "seem to throw off their beliefs as they pass through a University career; I made mine." Just before becoming an undergraduate he had, of his own accord, turned to the classics of religion and read them with the eagerness of one who is quenching a real and painful thirst. He read the Bible so earnestly as to draw from one of his friends the deliciously naïve remark "Toynbee reads his Bible like any other book—as if he liked it." In the course of his first year at Balliol he writes to a friend : "The two things the Bible speaks to our hearts most unmistakably are the unfathomable longing for God, and the forgiveness of sins; and these are the utterances that fill up an aching void in my secular religion—a religion which is slowly breaking to pieces under me. It is astonishing to think that in the Bible itself we find the most eloquent heart-rending expression of that doubt and utter darkness and disbelief which noisy rhetoricians and calm sceptics would almost persuade us were never before adequately expressed— they would tell us we must look for it all in their bald language." And a little later, "A speechless thrill of spiritual desire sometimes runs through me and makes me hope even when most weary." "As to position in life," he wrote about the same time, "the position I wish to attain to is that of a man consumed with the thirst after righteousness."

As Toynbee's religion had not come to him through the medium of customary religious forms, or in association with accepted religious dogmas, these dogmas and forms never were to him so momentous as they are to many devout souls. Not indeed that he was hostile to either. He knew that the practice of simple religious observances was beneficial to the spiritual life of the individual and necessary to the spiritual life of the nation; he joined in them and, as time went on, valued them more highly than he had done in youth. He would earnestly seek out the truth contained in accepted dogmas; but he could not help seeing how mischievous to religion and to civilization some of them have proved, and how inadequate all must necessarily be. His incisive intelligence and historical feeling forbade him to dress his faith in the worn out garb of mediæval devotion, or to try the spiritual discipline of believing what he knew to be untrue. Yet the same intelligence and feeling forbade him to set up an infinitesimal church of his own or to worship assiduously an ideal existing only in his own imagination. He thought that any follower of Christ might live in the Church of England. He always strove to find some definite intellectual conceptions to support his faith, for he saw that without such conceptions piety must degenerate into sentiment. It seemed to him that, whilst every age and country, nay every serious believer, must more or less differ in religious doctrine from every other, since religious doctrine is related to the whole spiritual, moral and intellectual life, which is infinitely various, yet doctrine of some kind or another is necessary in every instance, and peace and freedom are to be found, not in luxurious dreamy fiction, but in the humble acknowledgment that the best and highest utterances of man concerning God are inevitably imperfect, incoherent and transitory. Thus eagerly searching to har-

2

monize the piety which he had learned from the Bible, and the Imitation of Thomas à Kempis, with those modern ideas to which he was equally loyal, he found especial help in the teaching and conversation of the late Professor Green, whose lay sermons delivered in Balliol College made a memorable impression upon many who heard them. Professor Green united the critical temper of a German philosopher with the fervor of a Puritan saint. Between him and Toynbee there was an entire confidence and an intimate intellectual and spiritual communion which only death interrupted.

It would not be right here to set out a body of doctrine with Toynbee's name attached to it. He was ever feeling his way, seriving after truth, without arrogance, but with the honest resolution not to accept propositions merely because they flattered his higher sentiments. His nearest friends caught from his conversation, and still more from his daily life, a bright reflection of his inward fire; but none probably would venture to catalogue his beliefs. It will be better to try to gather from his own words what he really thought, always remembering that he was very young and oppressed by the immensity of religious conceptions. The following passage occurs in a letter written to an old schoolfellow who had become an officer and was then serving in the Indian Army. The letter is dated the 2nd of October, 1875, the first year of his residence at Balliol College:

" ' To love God '—those words gather amazing force as life gets more difficult, mysterious and unfathomable; one's soul in its loneliness at last finds religion the only clue. And yet how weary is the search for God among the superstitions, antiquities, contradictions and grossness of popular religion; but gleams of divinity are everywhere, and slowly in the end comes divine peace. . . . It seems to me that the primary element of all religion is the faith that the end for which the whole universe of sense and thought from the Milky Way to the lowest form of animal life, the end for which everything came into existence, is that the dim idea of perfect holiness which is found in the mind of man might be realized; that this idea is God Eternal and the only reality; that the relation between this idea which is God and each individual is religion, the consciousness of the relation creating the duty of perfect purity of inner life or being, and the duty of living for others, that they too may be perfectly pure in thought and action; and, lastly, that the world is so ordered that the triumph of righteousness is not impossible through the efforts of the individual will in relation to eternal existence. I speak of God as an idea and not as personal; I think you will understand what I mean if you ask yourself if the pure love and thoughts of a man are not all that makes his personality clear to you—whether you would care that anything else of him should be immortal; whether you do not think of all else of him as the mere expression and symbol of his eternal, invisible existence. My dear fellow, don't think it strange that I send you these bare, abstract thoughts all those dizzy leagues to India. I only want to tell you what I am thinking of; do not take heed of them except in so far as they chime harmoniously with your own belief; I think they are the truth, but truth comes to every mind so differently that very few can find the longed-for unity except in love."

From the passage just quoted the reader might draw an inference which it does not justify. Toynbee was perfectly well aware that a Divinity who is nothing more than an abstraction has never been and never can be the object of a real, living religion. Concerning the creed of the Positivists, whose virtues he honored, he wrote some years later. "Humanity is really an abstraction manufactured by the intellect; it can never be an object of religion, for religion in every form demands something that lives and is not made. It is the vision of a living thing that makes the Psalmist cry 'As the hart panteth after the water-brooks, so longeth my soul after thee, the living God.'" The following words quoted from an address upon the ideal relations of Church and State, may remove some doubts as to his own position:

"God is a person—how else could man love and worship God? What personality is, we only faintly apprehend—who has withdrawn the impenetrable veil which hides our own personality from us? God is a father—but who has explained a father's love? There is limitation to man's knowledge, and he is disposed to cry out, Why this impassable barrier? He knows he is limited—why he is limited he knows not. Only by some image does he strive to approach the mystery. The sea, he may say, had no voice until it ceased to be supreme on the globe. There, where its dominion ended and its limits began, on the edge of the land, it broke silence. Man would have had no tongue had he been merely infinite. Where he feels his limits, where the infinite spirit within him touches the shore of his finite life, there he, too, breaks silence."

On the other hand, all notions of a special Providence favoring this or that race, this or that individual, were shocking to Toynbee's moral and religious feelings. Nothing scandalized him more than the self-congratulation so often uttered by serious people on the occasion of their escape from the plagues and miseries which visit others. Miracles do not seem to have been felt by him as aids to the belief in God. The strangest of these supposed irregularities appeared to him less divine than the order and harmony of the universe. He might have chosen to express his feeling of the presence of God in the words of one of his favorite poets:

> "A sense
> Of something, far more deeply interfused,
> Whose dwelling is the light of setting suns,
> And the round ocean, and the living air,
> And the blue sky, and in the mind of man
> A motion and a spirit that impels
> All thinking things, all objects of all thought,
> And rolls through all things."

Not that his creed was pantheism, if by pantheism we mean merely a vague awe or admiration inspired by the mighty sum of existence. To him, as we have seen, God was a spirit, a

person in the fullest sense of the word. For him religion was inseparably bound up with conduct and with righteousness. "**If I** did not believe that the moral law was eternal," **he** once said, "**I** should die." But he felt irresistibly impelled to struggle out of the dualism which contents the multitude.

From weakness of imagination most religious people regard the visible world as something external to God, and related to Him only as a picture is related to the painter or as a kingdom is related to its sovereign. They find something reassuring and comforting in direct exertions of the Divine prerogative. As the inexplicable **is** for them the sacred, every expansion of their knowledge is a contraction **of** their faith. **Most** touching it **is** to hear them say, Ah! there are many **things for** which the men of science cannot account, many things which show that there must be a God. Most strange is their reluctant conviction that, in so far as the universe can be shown to be rational, it is proved to have no soul. Their frame of mind was quite impossible to Toynbee, who believed in science as he believed in God. He saw that the so-called conflict of religion and science really grows out of two intellectual infirmities common—the one among the devout multitude, the other among students of particular physical sciences. On the one hand, religious experiences have been almost inseparably associated in the popular mind with the belief in certain historical statements, which, whether true or false, must be tried by the critical canons applicable to all statements of that **kind.** On the other hand, absorption in the pursuit of physical science often leads men to forget that such science can give no ultimate explanation of anything, because it always postulates certain conceptions which it does not criticise. For facts of geology or biology we must always have recourse to geologists or to biologists, not because they know everything but because they alone can know anything relating **to** these sciences. **On** the other hand, neither the geologist nor the biologist, **as** such, can give the ultimate interpretation to be put upon **all** facts whatsoever. Free from these contending prejudices, Toynbee always felt sure that the progress of criticism must end, not in destroying religion, but in purifying religion from all that is **not** essential. Of the great Christian ideas he wrote: "They **are not** the creations of **a** particular hour and place, they are **universal,** but they became a compelling power owing to the inspiration of **one** teacher in a particular corner of **the** earth. What the real character of Christ was, what is the truth about certain incidents of his life, we may never ascertain, but the ideal Christ, the creation of centuries of Christian suffering and devotion, will be as little affected by historical scepticism as the character of Shakespeare's Hamlet by researches into the Danish chronicles. Prove to-morrow that the Scripture records and the Christian tradition are inventions and you would no more destroy their influence as a delineation of the spiritual life than the critics destroyed the spell of the Homeric poems by proving that Hector and Achilles never fought on the plains of Troy. This may seem a paradox, but the time will come when **we** shall no more think it necessary to agree with those who **assert** that Christianity must stand or fall **with** the resurrection of Christ than we now dream of saying with St. Bernard that it must stand or fall with belief in the Virgin Mary. The Christian records and the lives of the saints will be indispensable instruments for the cleansing of the spiritual vision, and the power which they exercise will be increased as their true value as evidence is understood. The Christian religion itself will in future rest upon a correct interpretation of man's spiritual character."

Toynbee was well aware of the spiritual languor which has been among the immediate results of the extraordinary growth of physical science in our own age. He had none the less a steadfast assurance that religion must in the end gain strength from the increase of knowledge. The following passage from an unpublished essay shows with what confidence he awaited the issue of that revolution in thought which has terrified so many good people :—

" Most terrible is the effect of the Reign of Law on the belief in immortality. Fever and despair come upon action, and the assertion that this world is all in all, narrows and perverts the world of ethical science. And, indeed, it is very awful, that great contrast of the Divine Fate of the world pacing on resistless and merciless, and our passionate individuality with its hopes and loves, and fears; that vision of our warm throbbing personal life quenched for ever in the stern sweep of Time. But it is but a passing picture of the mind; soon the great thought dawns upon the soul, 'It is I, this living, feeling man, that thinks of fate and oblivion; I cannot reach the stars with my hands, but I pierce beyond them with my thoughts, and if things go on in the illimitable depth of the skies which would shrivel up the imagination like a dead leaf, I am greater than they, for I ask "why" and look before and after, and draw all things into the tumult of my personal life—the stars in their courses, and the whole past and future of the universe, all things as they move in their eternal paths, even as the tiniest pool reflects the sun and the everlasting hills.'

" Like all great intellectual revolutions, the effect of the Reign of Law upon ethical temper has been harassing and disturbing; but as every great intellectual movement has in the end raised and ennobled the moral character of man through the purification of his beliefs, so will this great conception leave us the belief in God and the belief in immortality purified and elevated, strengthening through them the spirit of unselfishness which it is already beginning to intensify, and which makes us turn our faces to the future with an ever-growing hope."

Religion was the inspiring force of Toynbee's later years and his efforts to understand and contribute to the cure of social evils were prompted above all by the hope of raising the people to that degree of civilization in which a pure and rational religion would be possible to them. Sensitive to their physical sufferings he was in a degree which at times

almost overpowered his judgment; but he never imagined
that the franchise, regular employment at fair wages and
cheap necessaries were in themselves capable of appeasing
the tremendous cravings of human nature, of quieting the
animal appetites or of satisfying the nobler aspirations. He
did perceive, however, that a great number of our people live
in such a manner as to make materialism and fanaticism
almost unavoidable alternatives for them. Having found
religion for himself and being eager to help others to find it
he did not immediately become a missionary. He would
speak frankly of religion to those who appeared to him really
concerned about it; and he hoped that at some future time
he might find a way of preaching to the people. But it was
not in his nature to be loquacious about spiritual matters and
he was fond of quoting Bacon's saying: "The greatest of
atheists are the hypocrites; for they handle sacred things
without feeling them."

Toynbee's desire to understand and help the poor led him to
spend part of the vacations of 1875 in Whitechapel. Already
he had arrived at the conclusion that mere pecuniary assistance unaccompanied by knowledge and sympathy is not
enough to bring about any lasting change for the better in
their condition. But such knowledge and sympathy, he saw,
can only grow out of long and familiar intercourse, in which
both parties meet as nearly on an equality as the facts of the
case will allow. Acting upon these beliefs he took rooms in
a common lodging house in the Commercial Road, Whitechapel, and furnished them in the barest possible manner.
He cordially enlisted himself in the endeavors made by the
good people there to assist their neighbors. He always was
well aware of the value of existing organizations, of the fact
that the worst use which can be made of an institution is to
destroy it. He would have endorsed that fine saying of
Burke: "Wisdom cannot create materials; her pride is in
their use." He put himself at the disposal of the Reverend
Mr. Barnett, the Vicar of St. Jude's, and entered with zest

into all the little feasts and amusements of the school children and their teachers. He also worked under the Charity Organization Society, and particularly valued this employment as giving an incomparable insight into the real condition of those who are so much talkèd about and so little known. He also joined the Tower Hamlets Radical Club and spent many an evening there, trying to appreciate the ideas of East End politicians. Finding that many members of the club entertained especially strong prejudices upon the subjects of religion and of political economy, he chose these for his subjects when asked to address the club. In giving the address upon religion he discovered in himself a new power. Although he had not had any previous experience and had not elaborated his discourse beforehand, he spoke eagerly, clearly and continuously for nearly three-quarters of an hour and succeeded in fixing the attention of his hearers. He was thus led to the conclusion that speaking rather than writing would be the best medium for his ideas, and resolved to repeat the experiment as often as time and strength would allow. In substance, this address was an attempt to express, freed from accretions, the essence of religion, the thoughts and feelings common to the saints of all creeds and of all ages. When he sat down there followed a debate, more lively than orthodox in tone. One orator in particular derided the common conception of heaven as a place where the angels have nothing to do but to let their hair go on growing and growing for ever. His indefatigable industry, the noisy situation of his lodgings, the extreme dullness and dreariness of the east end of London, and, most of all, the constant spectacle of so much evil, so difficult, I will not say of cure, but of mitigation, made residence in Whitechapel too exhausting for Toynbee's delicate constitution. He never found fault with anything, and stuck to his post as long as he could. But he was at length forced to give up his experiment. Although he was never able to repeat it, it confirmed him in the belief that the prosperous must know before they can really assist the poor; and he was fond of insisting **that** thought and knowledge must now in philanthropy take **the** place of feeling. His example and teaching in this matter **have** resulted in the foundation of Toynbee Hall in Whitechapel, the inmates of which **are** enabled, without forsaking **their own** friends or pursuits, to live among those whom they wish **to benefit.**

Whilst thus busied with many things, Toynbee contrived to find delicious intervals of rest. He was a keen lover **of the** country. His naturally high spirits became almost boisterous in its pure air. Once or twice every year he escaped to some charming place, where with one or two friends and a few favorite books he revelled **in** pleasures that needed not to borrow from luxury. He preferred to all other beautiful districts **that of** the Lakes, endeared to him **by** memories of rambles enjoyed there in boyhood and by association with Wordsworth's poems. He **was** peculiarly sensitive to all charms of association. Beauty was to him rather suggestive than satisfying. He looked out upon the **world with the eyes of a** philosopher rather than that of an artist. **In the National** Gallery, one of his favorite haunts, he was fascinated less **by** revelations of perfect form and color than by the austere grace **and** pathos of such a painter as Francia. He was especially fascinated by the face of one of the angels in Francia's picture of the Entombment. "Shall I tell you to what I liken it?" he writes **in** a letter. "Have you on a still summer evening ever heard far-off happy human voices, and yet felt them **to** be sad because far-off? In this angel's face there is that happy **tone,** but so distant that you feel it **is also sad. Have** you ever, when the raindrops are pattering softly on the leaves, heard the sweet, low song of birds? In that angel's **face** are joy and sadness thus mingled." His travels in Italy in the year 1877 were to him full of interest and enjoyment; but Italy **does** not seem to have become dear to him; her art and her climate were perhaps felt by him as oppressively splendid; her sunny magnificence was not congenial to a temperament in its depths so full of seriousness.

He was a very accurate observer of outward things, and in his letters or conversation would reproduce with a fine touch the features of a remarkable landscape. He had learnt much from Mr. Ruskin's extraordinary descriptions of nature, but both by reading and by experiments of his own, had become convinced that the pictorial powers of language are narrowly limited. He saw that the mania for word-painting has for the most part resulted in verbosity, confusion and weakness. Writing to a friend, he observes:

"The best pieces of description are little bits of incidental observation. The worst are those interminable pages of mere word-daubing, which even Ruskin is not guiltless of. When you look for topographical accuracy, you are utterly disappointed. Since my interest in surface geology and physical geography has been sharpened by the study of political economy, I have looked out for plain facts in these fine rhapsodies, and have found them as useless as the purple mountains and luxuriant foregrounds of a conventional landscape. The fact is, a man must do one of two things. Either give a strict topographical account of a place, noting down relative heights and distances, conformation of the rocks, character of the vegetation, in such a way that you can piece the details together into an accurate outline; or he must generalize his description, carefully eliminating all local details and retaining only the general effect of the scene on his mind at the time. The greatest poets do the last; if you turn to the Allegro and Penseroso of Milton, you will be struck by the vividness of every touch and the absence of any attempt to picture an actual scene. In most modern descriptions there is a mixture of both kinds. You will find plenty of vague, often exaggerated expressions, confused by little pieces of irrelevant local detail which tease the imagination; they tell you a rose tree grew on the right side of the door, yet never give the slightest chance of placing yourself in the scene."

Unlike most travellers who, if they care for anything, care only for the picturesque, Toynbee was insatiable of information respecting the condition and way of thinking of the people amongst whom he travelled. So frank and cordial was he in his conversation with all sorts of men that all readily opened their minds to him. It is true that they took pains to show him as little as they could of their meanness or triviality, and it is probable that he, quick and eager as he was, sometimes read into their words thoughts which **were** not clearly there. Yet from this personal intercourse Toynbee derived knowledge which he could not have so well acquired in any other way. Young as he was, and almost overpowered by his feelings of benevolence and sympathy, he yet knew a great deal concerning the classes for whom he labored. In this respect he differed much from many good men of our own generation.

Indeed, notwithstanding his warm and enthusiastic devotion to the ideal and his indifference to the honors and rewards so highly valued by most of us, Arnold Toynbee had a great deal of common sense. He understood that if we cannot live by bread alone, neither can we subsist **solely on nectar** and ambrosia. One example of the prudence which he exercised, **at** least in counselling others if not always for himself, may be quoted here. A younger brother, having gone into business **in** the City, was oppressed with a growing distaste for his work and for his companions. He began to think seriously of choosing another walk in life, and took counsel with Arnold. Arnold, in reply, wrote as follows:

" I am very sorry you are so disappointed with your work. What you say about the habits and tastes of business men is, no doubt, true; but don't imagine that other classes are very different. If you came here and went to a small college, you would find that the tastes and habits of the majority of undergraduates were much the same as the tastes and habits of clerks in the City. I **say** a small college, because in large colleges, where you have greater numbers to choose from, you would find a certain number like yourself, who care for refinement and dislike coarseness: but you would have to pick them out. Remember, refinement is not common. In no occupation which you wished to adopt would you find the ways and opinions of your fellows, or most of them, those which you have been brought up to seek and approve. Don't misunderstand me. All I mean to say is, human nature in the City is much like human nature in the University. The passions of men who cast up accounts and buy and sell tea are not very unlike the passions of men who study Plato and struggle for University distinctions. Whatever work you undertake, you must expect to have to do with coarse men who pursue low aims. You will, perhaps, answer: 'But in this case there is literally not a single person I care for or can make my friend. In another occupation there would, at least, be one or two men I could like.'

"Granting this, let me advise you on one point—don't think of throwing up your present work, until you see quite clearly what other work there is you can do which will suit you better and enable you to make a livelihood. Look about, make enquiries, but don't allow yourself to change until you have fixed on some new line and fixed it after fullest consideration of all you will have to face.

"People who have no decided bent for any one thing, naturally think that whatever they undertake is not the work they are best fitted for; this is true of a great many people. If you can point to anything you would like to do better than anything else—I should say, do it at once, if you can get a livelihood by it. As it is, I say, wait, be patient, make the best of your work, and be glad you have the refinement you miss in other people.

"There—I hope you don't think I am harsh. I know your position is difficult, is unpleasant—but I don't see how it can be altered yet, and therefore I advise you to do what I am sure you can do—make the best of it.

"Ever your loving brother,

"A. TOYNBEE."

The author of this wise and sententious letter had said in one written some time before, "As a rule we find our friends and counsellors anywhere but in our own family." The saying, although a hard one, is true; and the explanation given is ingenious. "We are so near and so alike in many things, we brothers and sisters, that in certain details we have a more intimate knowledge of each other's characters than our dearest friends. We know the secret of every little harsh accent or selfish gesture; words that seem harmless to others are to us full of painful meaning because we know too well in ourselves the innermost folds of the faults they exprsss. There is nothing we hate more than our own faults in others; that is the reason why so many brothers are in perpetual feud, why so many sisters are nothing to each other, why whole families live estranged. And yet it is equally obvious that a chance acquaintance often judges us more fairly than our own nearest relations, because these details worked into prominence by the trying friction of everyday life, are after all only a very small part of us which our relations rarely see in perspective. That is the reason. Though near in some ways, we are never far enough off. We never see each other's characters in proportion, as wholes."

III.

Having taken his degree, Toynbee had next to consider how he should secure a livelihood. He had come up to Oxford without definite prospects and during his stay there had become more and more unwilling to adopt any of the ordinary professions. He had not gained those distinctions or accumulated that sort of knowledge which may be said to ensure election to a fellowship. He had, however, impressed the authorities of Balliol College with his rare gifts of talent and character; and by them he was appointed tutor to the students at that college who were qualifying themselves for the Indian Civil Service. The performance of the duties attached to his post left him a good deal of leisure in which to prosecute his favorite studies. The stipend was not large, but he was a man of few wants and always held simplicity of life to be a sacred duty. He was not without desires, but they were impersonal, and besides were under the control of a strong will. Always delicate and often suffering from severe illness, he had never acquired the habit of petting himself. He had retained all the manliness which we usually fancy inseparable from robust health. Yet, whilst thus severe towards himself, he was indulgent to others, generous, spirited and quite free from those boorish or cynical oddities which have so often deformed the appearance and conversation of men distinguished by unworldliness. In his countenance, in his words, in his tastes, in his actions, there was a distinction and an elegance which preserved his simplicity from plainness. There was something in his presence which checked impertinence and frightened vulgarity.

Had Arnold Toynbee lived in the thirteenth century, he would probably have entered or founded a religious order, unless he had been first burnt for a heretic. In the nineteenth century, he lived to show how much may be done, nay, how much may be enjoyed by a man whom society would think poor. When about to address audiences of workingmen, mostly artisans and mechanics, he used to say that he liked to think he was not himself much richer than they were. True, there was just the least touch of exaggeration in his scorn of superfluities. His ideas respecting the income sufficient for keeping a house and rearing a family sometimes forced a smile from those more versed in the sordid struggles of the world and in the sad defacement of human nature which those struggles cause. These ideas, however, influenced his political creed. He always believed in the possibility of a democratic society, whose members should be intellectual, refined, nay spiritual; and, believing in this possibility, he joyfully hailed the spread of democratic institutions. Perhaps he did not fully realize the enormous cost and trouble required in most instances for the full development of human faculties. Perhaps he did not quite understand how deep-rooted in the necessity of things is the frantic eagerness of all men of all classes and parties to seize the means of life and expansion. Carlyle's comparison of mankind to a pot of tamed Egyptian vipers, each trying to get its head above the others, was foreign to his way of thinking. Men's generous instincts and high aspirations he shared and therefore understood; but their imperious appetites and sluggish consciences he had only studied from without; he had not learnt by communing with his own soul. Like Milton, Shelley or Mazzini, totally dissociated from the vulgar wants of the upper, the lower or any other class, he was a democrat, because he contemned the riches and honors of this world, not because he was anxious to secure for himself as much thereof as fell to the lot of any other man.

In June of the year 1879 Toynbee married a lady who had for several years been his close friend. She survives to mourn an irreparable loss, and it would not be fitting to say of their married life more than this that it was singularly happy and beautiful. During the few months immediately following upon his marriage Toynbee seemed to regain much of the health and elasticity proper to his time of life. The pleasure of finding himself understood by the person whom of all others he most valued and the calming influence of a regular occupation had a most wholesome effect upon his highly strung and over-taxed nerves. His constitution seemed to recruit itself daily in the genial atmosphere of a home. His spirits became higher and more equable than they had been for many years. His thoughts grew clearer and clearer to him. It seemed, alas! it only seemed that he was about to rise out of the pain and weakness of youth, and to enter upon a long career of beneficent industry. Too soon this fair prospect was clouded. He plunged with redoubled ardor into endless and multifarious labors. He found so much to do, he was so eager to do it all, that he would never seek rest and so at

length **rest** would not come to **him.** He felt his intellectual
power grow day by day and could not or would not own that
day by day its working frayed more and more the thread of
the thin-spun life.

He had never lost his early preference for quiet study.
Although he had relinquished history and the philosophy of
history in favor **of** political economy, he remained by the
bent of his mind an historian. He had learnt much from
the economic writings of Cliffe Leslie which are distinguished
by the constant use of the historical method ; but he saw that
without the help of deduction, this method can serve only to
accumulate **a mass of** unconnected and unserviceable **facts.**
He did full **justice to** the logical power displayed in the
economic writings of John Stuart Mill and Cairnes. It is
the more necessary to bear this in mind because in his essay
upon "Ricardo and the Old Political Economy" he **assailed**
their spiritual father with somewhat of youthful **vehemence**
and even styled the Ricardian system an intellectual impos-
ture. He felt very strongly that our English economists had
made, not too much use of logic, but too little use of history,
and, by constructing their theories upon too narrow a basis of
fact, had lessened as well the value as the popularity of their
science. He saw that these theories needed correction and
re-statement. He would not have denied their partial truth
nor **would he have echoed the** newspaper nonsense about
political economy having been banished to the planet Saturn.
Here as in so many other instances his intellectual fairness
and love of truth checked **a** sensibility **as keen as that of**
Owen or Ruskin.

He was anxious **to** make some worthy contribution **to**
economic literature, and finally chose for his subject the industrial revolution in England. Considering the magnitude
of that revolution, which turned feudal and agricultural into
democratic **and** commercial England, it is somewhat surpris-
ing that its history should have remained unwritten to this
day. For Toynbee it had a peculiar fascination. During the

3

last two years of his life he accumulated a great deal of
material for the work and made original investigations upon
several points, especially upon the decline of the yeomanry.
Part of the knowledge thus amassed he gave out in a course
of lectures delivered in Balliol College ; and from the notes
of these lectures the fragments which have been published
were collected. Few and broken, indeed, they are; yet full
of unavailing promise. Other economists have shown greater
dialectical power; but none have made a happier use of historical illustration. He had the faculty of picking out from
whole shelves of dusty literature the few relevant facts.
These facts he could make interesting because he never lost
sight of their relation to life. Political economy was always
for him a branch of politics, in the nobler sense of that term ;
the industrial revolution but a phase of a vaster and more
momentous revolution, touching all the dearest interests of
man.

The problems suggested by a competitive system of society
were always present to his mind. He felt as deeply as any
socialist could feel the evils incidental to such a system, the
suffering which it often brings upon the weak, the degradation
which it often brings about in the strong. For the cure of
these evils, however, he looked further than most socialists
do. Owning that competition was a mighty and, in some
respects, a beneficent power, he wrote that " of old it was
hindered and controlled by custom ; in the future, like the
other great physical forces of society, it will be controlled by
morality." To the same effect is the following passage : " In
the past all associations had their origin in unconscious physical motives ; in the future all associations will have their
origin in conscious ethical motives. Here, as in so many
other things, the latest and most perfect development of
society seems to be anticipated in its outward form by the
most primitive; only the inner life of the form has changed."
In the meantime, he held with John Stuart Mill that the
problem of distribution was the true problem of political

economy at the present day. Certainly it was the problem which most interested him, and his way of handling it was characteristic. With the habit of forming somewhat startling ideals, he had the instinct of scientific investigation. Convinced that feeling, however pure or intense, is not alone equal to the improvement of society, he was always toiling to find in the study of that which is, the key to that which ought to be. He would bury himself in the dry details of an actual economic process, and emerge only to suggest in the soberest terms some modest but practicable amelioration. This singularly positive side of his enthusiastic nature is illustrated by the letter to Mr. Thomas Illingworth of Bradford, which is printed at the end of this memoir.

Toynbee's interest in the welfare of mankind was too eager and impatient to be satisfied solely by the pursuit of truth. He was zealous for that diffusion of political knowledge which halts so immeasurably behind the diffusion of political power. He felt that even now, in spite of better education and greater opportunities of reading, the bulk of the nation scarcely partakes in the progress of science. The growing wealth of recorded experience, the enlargement and correction of thought are real only to a few students who exercise almost no direct influence upon the course of public affairs, whilst public men who do exercise this influence are so enslaved to the exigencies of each passing day that they have little time or strength to spare for the education of their followers. Toynbee was anxious to utilize for political reform the ferment of thought at the Universities. With this purpose he drew together into an informal society several of the most studious among his younger contemporaries. Each member was to select for his special study some principal department of politics, but all were to work in concert, and to maintain, by meeting from time to time for discussion, a general level of sympathy and information. When they had matured their views they were to take part in forming public opinion by writing or by speaking as best suited each man's talent and opportunities. The conception of such a society had long been familiar to him and this was not his first attempt to carry it out. He would dwell mournfully on that practical impotence of clever and earnest University men which has afforded so much matter for exultation to the enemies of polite letters. "Every one is organized," he wrote, "from licensed victuallers to priests of the Roman Catholic Church. The men of wide thought and sympathies alone are scattered and helpless."

The society held its first meeting in the June of 1879 and continued for three years to meet once a term, sometimes in London, but oftener in Oxford. As time went on it was joined by one or two younger men who shared the studies and aims of the original members. Toynbee was throughout the guiding and animating spirit. **Deep differences** of opinion necessarily came to light, but those who differed most from Toynbee would be the first to confess **how much** they have learnt from discussion with him. **So penetrating** was his earnestness, so thorough his dialectic, that the faculties of all who listened to him were strained to the utmost. All were forced to ask themselves what they really believed and **why they** believed it. Toynbee was anxious that these debates **should** not prove merely academic; and he and his friends spent some time in considering how they could best preach their doctrines. He himself had a gift of addressing large audiences; but this gift is rare, and it is hard to find any other mode of communicating new ideas to the people. **A** volume of essays can only be published at a considerable cost; pamphlets are scarcely read at all; and a newspaper can **be** floated only by those who have considerable capital or are totally subservient to a political party. In this as in all other efforts to diffuse enlightenment we have to shift as best we can; put forth our opinions when we get a chance and not expect any one else to mind them.

Toynbee had not forgotten his own success in addressing the Tower Hamlets Radical Club. He was resolved to use the power which he had then found himself to possess in communicating to the artisans of our great towns the ideas **which he** had matured in the quiet of Oxford. It was his design to give every year a certain number of lectures upon such economic problems as were of the most pressing practical importance to workingmen. These lectures were not to be merely academic or merely partisan. They were to combine the directness and liveliness of a party harangue with the precision and fairness of a philosophical discourse. He knew how prejudiced against political economy are the poor; but he knew that mistakes made by economists have helped to strengthen that prejudice, and he believed that it would yield to frankness and sympathy. He believed that the masses were eager for illumination—that they would be delighted to follow any intelligent man of whose sincerity and disinterestedness they felt assured. He used to refer to the success which had attended Mr. Bradlaugh's lectures and to the influence which they had exerted, and would urge that other preachers with equal courage and faith might gain a greater success and wield a far better influence.

It was in the January of 1880 that Toynbee began his series of popular addresses by giving at Bradford three lectures upon Free Trade, the Law of Wages and England's Industrial Supremacy. He did not write out his lectures beforehand nor did he speak from notes; but having mastered his subject by intense thought, trusted for fitting words to the inspiration of the moment. This practice, whilst it increased the fatal strain upon his nervous system, added much to the grace and naturalness of his delivery. From the faces of expectant listeners he drew the needful stimulus to his power of expression. He spoke rapidly and continuously, yet with clearness and accuracy. He carried away his audience, and their momentum carried him swiftly and smoothly to the close. At Bradford his lectures were well attended and well received by both employers and workmen. He was always anxious to address both classes together and

not separately, for with him it was a prime object to soften
the antagonism between capital and labor, to show that the
true, the permanent, interests of both are identical. **The**
address upon Wages and Natural **Law he** subsequently delivered again at Firth College, Sheffield, and **it has** been reprinted
from the shorthand writer's reports. Such an address cannot
be expected to contain much abstruse or recondite speculation.
It illustrates very happily, however, the constant drift of his
economic teaching. It enforces Mill's distinction between the
laws of production, which are laws of nature uncontrollable
by our will, and the laws of distribution, which are, to a considerable extent, the result of human contrivance, and may be
amended with the growth of intelligence and fairness. Thus,
it points out that the earlier economists arrived at their conception of a wages fund by leaving out of account many of
the causes which affect the rate of wages, by forgetting that it
is not competition alone that determines the rate of wages;
that trades unions, that custom, that law, that public opinion,
that the character of employers all influence wages—that their
rate is not governed by an inexorable law, nor determined
alone by what a great writer once termed "the brute law of
supply and demand." This address is also remarkable for a
candor uncommon in those who profess themselves friends
and advocates of the working classes. Such persons seldom
address their clients without slipping into a style of flattery.
Toynbee, who loved the people with all his heart and was,
perhaps, prejudiced in their favor, avoided this pernicious
cant. He reminded his hearers that a rise in wages was
desirable in the interests of the whole community only in so
far as **it** led to a rise in the civilization of the wage-earners.
"You know only too well," he said, "that too many workingmen do not know how to use the wages which they have at
the present time. You know, too, that an increase of wages
often means an increase of crime. If workingmen are to
expect their employers to act with larger notions of equity in
their dealings in the labor market, it is, at least, rational that

. employers should expect that workingmen shall set about
reforming their own domestic life. It is, at least, reasonable
that they should demand that workingmen shall combine to
put down drunkenness and brutal sports." Coming from **a**
speaker whose affection was unquestionable, sentences such as
the above were taken in good part by the workmen who
heard them. Toynbee never found that he lessened his popularity by abstaining from adulation of the people.

In the course of January and February, 1881, **he** delivered
twice, once at Newcastle and once at Bradford, the lecture
entitled "Industry **and** Democracy." This lecture **was a**
study of one **aspect of** that great industrial revolution **which**
was ever present to his thoughts. Its central idea may **be**
roughly stated as follows. A series of extraordinary mechanical inventions extending over the latter half of the eighteenth
century shattered the old industrial organization of England
and in particular broke the bond of protection and dependence
which formerly united the employer and the employed. But
some time elapsed before the revolution in the industrial **was**
followed by the revolution in the political system. Some
time elapsed before the workman's economic isolation was followed by **his** political enfranchisement. He had lost his
patron and he was slow in learning to help himself. This
interval was for him a period of suffering and for the whole
body politic a period of danger. But this epoch of dissolu-
tion has been followed by **an** epoch of **new** combinations.
The workmen have organized themselves **for** their economic
and social advancement; and **they** have acquired the fullest
political status. They are **now** independent citizens with
ampler rights and duties than could have **been** theirs in the
old-fashioned industrial and political order; and thus in England, at least, the acutest crisis of the double revolution,
political and economical, has been surmounted, and an age of
tranquil development has become possible. Such is the bare
outline of **an** address abounding in knowledge and in thought,
which fixed the attention of very large audiences.

A year later he gave at Newcastle, Bradford and Bolton an
address upon the question—"Are Radicals Socialists?" This
was one of the many attempts that have been made to settle
the true line of separation between the functions which must
be discharged by the state and the functions which may be
discharged by the individual. It proposed three tests whereby to try the wisdom of interference in any particular instance
by the state: "first, the matter must be one of primary social
importance; next, it must be proved to be practicable; thirdly,
the state interference must not diminish self-reliance." It
will probably occur to all who have pursued inquiries of this
nature that the hardest thing is, not to lay down good rules,
but to insure their observance. In our age, at least, it is not
so much want of knowledge as the zeal of narrow enthusiasts
or the interested ambition of political intriguers which leads
to an excessive or injudicious interference by the state with
the individual.

These were not the only addresses which Toynbee gave in
pursuance of his favorite plan; but they have been singled
out here, because they have been reprinted among his literary
remains and are characteristic both in thought and expression.
They are all pervaded by a hopefulness heightened, perhaps,
by youth, yet innate in the man. Toynbee thought that the
conditions for solving the question of the relation between
capital and labor were to be found, if in any country, in England. The old habit of joint action for public ends by men
of every class; the ennobling traditions of freedom and order;
the strong sense and energetic moderation often displayed by
the workmen, particularly in the north, their experience
acquired in organizing and administering trades unions and
co-operative societies; and the large mass of property already
held by them; all these circumstances convinced him that, in
England at least, an even and steady progress was possible, if
men of culture and public spirit would offer themselves to
lead the way. He saw that the laboring classes have political
power sufficient to insure the most serious and respectful con-

sideration of their demands and he trusted that the consciousness of this power and the spread of education would awaken
in them something of that national feeling, that devotion to
the interests of the state which has never yet been wanting in
any age of our history. If in all this he was too sanguine,
yet was his illusion a noble one which tended to verify itself.
Could politicians or journalists ever address workingmen without trying either to bribe or to flatter them, we may be assured
that workingmen would respond to something else beside
bribes or flattery. It should be added that for these lectures he never took any remuneration beyond his travelling
expenses, and not always this.

Of all the means employed by the poor to better their
condition, the co-operative system appeared to him the most
effectual. This system, we know, has proved more successful
in distribution than in production; but it is capable of indefi-
nite expansion in the hands of intelligent and honest men.
Toynbee hoped that it might come to include a teaching
organization. In the winters of 1880 and the following
years, he used to lecture on political economy to a class of
workingmen, which met at the Oxford Co-operative Stores.
Sometimes he would have his hearers at his house on Sunday
evenings and engage them in general conversation on economic
subjects. In the course of his work with this class he formed
many friendships with individual workmen, who regarded him
with real devotion. They may still be heard to say, " We
thought he would have done so much for us and for the town."
"He understood us," they would say, "he took up things and
led us in a way there seems no one else to do." Toynbee
used also to contribute to the Oxford Co-operative Record.
In a paper written for that periodical, entitled "Cheap Clothes
and Nasty," he urged the workingmen to remember what hard
and ill-requited labor, the labor, too, of their own class and
their own kindred, was required to produce their cheap cloth-
ing. "The great maxim we have all to follow," he wrote,
" is that the welfare of the producer is as much a matter of

interest to the consumer as the price of the product;" wise
and true words, how seldom borne in mind. At the Whit-
suntide of 1882, when the co-operative societies held at Oxford
their annual congress, he read a more elaborate paper upon
"The Education of Co-operators." He showed how needful
and how much neglected at the present time is the education of men as citizens, and suggested that the co-operative
societies might well provide for the civic education of their
own members. He then sketched a programme of political
and economical instruction. This programme may be thought
ambitious; yet the address as a whole is singularly balanced
and judicial. He was well aware that there were many
obstacles in the way of carrying out that which he proposed,
and that the greatest of these obstacles is not the difficulty
of finding competent teachers, nor the expense of employing
them, but the apathy of those who were to be instructed.
Such apathy he recognized as natural in men tired out with
toil; but although natural, not the less baneful. "Languor,"
he truly said, "can only be conquered by enthusiasm, and
enthusiasm can only be kindled by two things: an ideal
which takes the imagination by storm, and a definite intelligible plan for carrying out that ideal into practice." In this
sentence he unconsciously summed up his own career. His
own enthusiasm was not of the heart only, but of the whole
man; it was a reflective enthusiasm with definite aims and
definite means; and for this reason it did not pass away like
the sentimental enthusiasms of so many generous young men;
on the contrary, as he grew older, it deepened until it became
a consuming fire.

The duties of a Balliol College tutor, the study of a com-
plicated science, the labors of a public lecturer upon political
and social questions; these might surely have been enough to
task the energies of a delicate man who at his best could only
work a few hours a day and was liable to frequent intervals
of forced inaction. Yet there was another task from which
Toynbee could not withhold his hand, a task which for him

comprised all others. Religion, it has been said, was the supreme interest of his life. His mode of thinking about religion has been hinted at above. He had too real a devotion to find repose in the worship of an abstract noun or an abstract sentiment. He felt that the religious emotion, like all other emotions, must have a real and an adequate object. He saw distinctly the weakness which has so often paralyzed the spiritual influence of the Broad Church. "Had liberal theologians in England combined more often with their undoubted courage and warmth, definite philosophic views, religious liberalism would not now be condemned as offering nothing more than a mere sentiment of vague benevolence. Earnest and thoughtful people are willing to encounter the difficulty of mastering some unfamiliar phrases of technical language, when they find they are in possession of a sharply defined intellectual position upon which their religious faith may rest."

Thus Toynbee, whilst in full sympathy with the modern critical spirit which regards as provisional all dogmas, even those which it may itself accept, was equally in sympathy with the instinct of devotion which in all ages has tried to find for itself a suitable dogmatic expression. The intellectual conceptions which support our spiritual life must always be inadequate and therefore variable; indeed they vary from land to land, from generation to generation, from class to class of a nation, from year to year in the life of the individual. But imperfect as these conceptions must be at any given time or place, they cannot be summarily remodelled; for they are the outcome of a vast experience, of an almost interminable intellectual history. They are improved sometimes by direct and severe criticism; oftener by the general growth of civilization and increase of knowledge. What is true of doctrine is likewise true of discipline and of ceremonies. All three have had a. long development. The various Churches now existing in our own country are full of faults; but they cannot be swept away at a stroke, nor, if they could, would there be anything better to take their place. To Toynbee a Church, like a State, was a mighty historical institution, the result of desires, hopes, beliefs which only in building it up could have found their satisfaction. Like a State, a Church had grown to be what it was and might grow to be something much better. How, he asked himself, could a devout man, totally without sectarian prejudice, assist even by a little that almost imperceptible growth? Certainly the survey of the state of religion in England at the present time does not readily suggest an answer to this question. Confusion is everywhere. We see many men of strong and cultivated intelligence, no longer obliged to fight for spiritual freedom, lapsing into an epicurean indifference, the more profound because it is so thoroughly goodnatured. This indifference is no longer confined to a few polished sceptics. It is shared by possibly the **greater part** of those who live by manual labor. It is not **rare among** women, always slower than men to part from the creed of their forefathers. A sincere piety is still common among us, but this piety, **too** often unenlightened, is frequently a principle of discord. Many zealous priests and laymen of the Established Church seem intent upon developing everything that is least rational in her doctrine, least sober and manly in her ritual. The Nonconformists, earnest as they are, seem condemned by their passionate spirit of division to everlasting pettiness and sterility. The Church of Rome, now as heretofore, invites, often with success, the timid and devout to abjure all the truths and all **the** liberties won in the battle of the last six centuries and to immure their souls in her dogmatic cloister. Look where we may, we nowhere behold realized the complete ideal of a national church. Religion, ceasing **to** be national, has lost half its life and power. Any reformation which is to restore its vigor must render **it** national once more.

For such a reformation the Church of England as by law established offers more facilities than any other. National it is, not only as the largest religious community in the kingdom,

but also as acknowledging in every Englishman a right to its
ministrations, in having for its head the head of the state, and
in admitting of regulation by the Imperial Parliament. Its
history has always been linked with the history of the nation.
If in former times it abused its power, it is at the present day
tolerant and open to ideas to an extent unparalleled in the
history of religion. It embraces members of the most various,
not to say, contradictory opinions; and this fact, so often cited
as its disgrace, is really its glory, since in a free and critical
age no **two thinking men** can word for word subscribe the
same creed. **The only** church possible in modern times is
a church whose members, whilst several in thought, **yet**
remain united in piety. The Catholics are **not** mistaken
when they insist upon the power which springs from unity;
the Nonconformists are in the right when they insist upon the
freedom and the responsibility of the individual soul. **The**
Church of England has endeavored, weakly indeed and inter-
mittently, to reconcile unity with freedom. It has been **able**
to do so because it has been a state church. The service **of**
the state is perfect freedom as compared with the yoke of the
priest or the yoke of the coterie. All **that was** best in the
Church of **England** appeared to Toynbee indissolubly linked
with **her alliance with the state.** Viewing **the** state as something **more than a mechanical** contrivance for material ends,
as **a union of men** for the highest purposes of human nature,
he did **not regard it as** inferior to the church or think the
church **degraded by connection** with the state. The church
and the state were to him but different aspects of the same
society. Like his friend Thomas Hill **Green he felt an**
intense antipathy to the pretensions of the sacerdotal party
who understand by the freedom of the church the domina-
tion of the clergy. He felt an equally strong antipathy for
the tyranny over thought and action exercised by the petty
majorities in what are known as the free churches. He
believed that real religious freedom was only possible in a
national church, and that **there** could be no national church

without the assistance of the state. But he acknowledged that the Church of England cannot be truly national until she gives self-government to her congregations and releases her ministers from subscription.

To effect these changes had been the object of the Church Reform Union, formerly organized by Mr. Thomas Hughes and the Reverend Mr. Llewelyn Davies, but then in a rather sleepy condition. Toynbee tried to give it fresh life and induced these gentlemen to reopen the discussion of church reform. He persuaded several of his friends to join the Union and organized an Oxford branch, besides writing leaflets to enlist the sympathy of the laboring classes. He went so far as to appear at the Church Congress held at Leicester in the year 1880, and to deliver an address upon the subject of Church Reform. Had his life been prolonged, he might have achieved much for the cause. The eloquent enthusiasm with which he used to dwell upon the ideal relations of Church and State made a deep impression upon men of very different religious beliefs. The impression cannot be reproduced in words, because it was originally due to something unspoken and indefinable in the man. Something of the spirit in which he approached the question may be caught from the following passage :—

"To teach the people, the ministers of religion must be independent of the people, to lead the people, they must be in advance of the people. Individual interests are not always public interests. It is the public interest that a country should be taught a pure and spiritual religion; it is the interest of religious teachers to teach that which will be acceptable at the moment. It is for the public interest that religion should be universal, that it should be a bond of union, that it should be progressive. The State, and not the individual, is best calculated to provide such a religion. We saw before that freedom being obtained, it was religion that was to weld free but isolated beings into a loving interdependent whole. Which is the more likely to do this—a religion wise and rational, comprehensive and universal, recognizing a progressive revelation of God, such as the State may provide, or a religion provided by individual interests which is liable to become what is popular at the moment, which accentuates and multiplies divisions, which perpetuates obsolete forms, and has no assurance of universality of teaching? It is scarcely too much to say that as an independent producer can only live by satisfying physical wants in the best way, the independent sect or independent minister can only live by satisfying spiritual wants in the worst way. If I thought that disestablishment were best for the spiritual interests of the people, I would advocate it, but only on such a principle can it be justified, and my argument is, that spiritual evil, not good, would attend it.

" What is really required is a body of independent ministers in contact at once with the continuous revelation of God in man, and in nature, and with the religious life of the people. The State alone can establish such a church organization as shall insure the independence of the minister, by securing him his livelihood and protecting him from the spiritual despotism of the people. I believe the argument holds good for religion as for education, that it is of such importance to the State itself, to the whole community collectively, that it behoves the State not to leave it to individual effort, which, as in the case of education, either does not satisfy spiritual wants at all, or does not satisfy them in the best way. If I chose to particularize, I might here add that the connection of religion with the State is the most effective check to sacerdotalism in all its different forms, and sacerdotalism is the form of religion which can become fundamentally dangerous to the State. It injures the State spiritually by alienating the greatest number and the most intellectual of the members of the State from religion altogether; it injures the State temporally by creating an antagonism between Church and State—a great national calamity from which we are now entirely free."

It must not be concluded from the above quotation that Toynbee regarded as just or expedient the present impotence

of the laity of the Church of England. He would have been
in favor of investing each congregation with almost any power
short of the power to dismiss its minister at discretion ; but
he thought that the ultimate control of the Church was more
safely vested in a democratic Parliament than in the inhabitants of each parish. In the same spirit of compromise he
would have abolished "clerical subscription," the formal
declaration of assent to the Articles and the teaching of the
English Book of Common Prayer, which is demanded from
every minister of the Established Church. It might have
been objected to him that, by abolishing "subscription," the
clerical profession is thrown open to men of every religion
and of no religion. He might have replied that the only
practical consequence of enforcing "subscription" is to exclude
from the ministry a few delicately spiritual natures, who
honor it too much to begin their professional life with
solemnly assenting to a series of obscure propositions drawn
up by the statesmen of the sixteenth century. Nevertheless,
we must allow that Toynbee failed fully to comprehend the
difficulty of his undertaking. He had found his religion for
himself, and it was all the more real to him because freed
from everything which was not spiritual. He could not,
therefore, realize the extravagant value which most of the
members of every Church attach to the accidents of their
spiritual life, especially to all modes of doctrine, ritual or
government which serve to distinguish them from other
Churches. Men are most partial to that which is distinct-
ively their own. Let it be trivial, unmeaning, mischievous,
still it is theirs, and, as such, sacred. The smallest concessions upon the part of the Established Church would often
have hindered the rise of new sects. The differences which
divide most sects from one another and from the Established
Church are, in many cases, too small for the naked eye, and
intelligible only when subjected to the historic microscope.
It does not follow that these concessions would have been
easy—that those differences can now be healed.

Whilst brooding over ideals of Church and State, Toynbee was always ready to lavish time and thought in furthering the welfare of his immediate neighbors. In devotion to the welfare of the city of Oxford, he rivalled his friend Professor Green. In the year 1881 he was appointed to the board of "Guardians of the Poor." The granting of relief, except within the walls of the workhouse, he had always condemned on the ground that it tended to lower wages and to relax industry; and when he became a guardian he uniformly acted upon this opinion. At the same time he felt the cruelty of compelling the deserving poor to take refuge in the workhouse, and the necessity of replacing "outdoor" relief by organized charity, which should assist them in the most effectual manner and make between the givers and receivers a bond of kindness and of gratitude. He therefore joined the committee of the Oxford Branch of the Charity Organization Society, thus helping to establish a concert between the public and the private relief of distress. He took extraordinary trouble in the investigation of cases of poverty and in securing uniformity and thoroughness in the operations of the Society. Nothing more enhanced the regard felt for him by the working men of Oxford than did these labors. They were indeed too much for one so weak in body and so heavily burthened with other employments. But he felt the necessity of not merely conceiving and uttering, but also in some small degree executing fine ideas. As a Christian and a citizen he thought himself in conscience bound to take his share of social drudgery, and to this austere sense of duty he sacrificed the few hours of rest which he so much needed, the scanty remains of strength which might have been employed in so many other ways more likely to bring fame and power. It was the reward of Toynbee's thoroughly sincere and practical spirit that he was always learning. His imagination was ever prone to pass beyond the bounds of possibility; but his habit of action constantly checked the disposition to reverie.

In spite of all the public labors which he had imposed upon

4

himself he took the utmost pains with his pupils, the selected candidates for the Indian Civil Service. He chiefly taught them political economy and could not go very deeply into that subject, because with them it was one of a multitude in which they had to be examined. But feeling how enormous a responsibility would hereafter rest upon these lads he diligently studied the recent history and present condition of our Indian Empire. He did what he could to quicken their sense of the great interests committed to their charge. Nor did he fail to cultivate those kindly personal relations between tutor and pupil which are so precious an element in the life of the University. Besides his tutorship he held for some time before his death the office of senior bursar to Balliol College. In this character he made the acquaintance of the tenants of the College estates, with whom he speedily became popular. The work interested him as affording a practical knowledge of the state of agriculture. So highly did the College value his services in this and in every other capacity that it was resolved to elect him a Fellow, and the resolution was defeated only by his untimely death.

With such a variety of occupations Toynbee was not able to take many holidays in the years following his marriage. In the summer of 1880 he had spent five delightful weeks in Switzerland, and on his return journey had stopped at Mulhausen to inspect its cotton factories and *cité ouvrière*— a town of model houses for the operatives, which they might acquire in perpetuity by gradual payments. Part of the summer of 1882 he spent in Ireland, but this was not for him a time of rest. He used his utmost endeavors to become acquainted with the true state of the peasantry, would stop them by the wayside or sit for hours in their cabins listening to endless talk. Eager and excitable as he was, he could not use his intelligence without agitating his feelings. On his way home he made the acquaintance of Mr. Michael Davitt, who seems to have been deeply impressed with Toynbee's conversation. Mr. Davitt subsequently wrote when sending a contribution to the Memorial Fund :

" I had the pleasure of making the acquaintance of the late
Mr. A. Toynbee during his Irish tour, as well as the advantage of a subsequent correspondence, and few men have ever
impressed me so much with being possessed of so passionate a
desire to mitigate the lot of human misery. In his death this
unfortunate country has lost one thoroughly sincere English
friend and able advocate, who, had he lived, would have
devoted some of his great talents to the task of lessening his
countrymen's prejudice against Ireland."

During the three terms from October, 1881, to June, 1882,
Toynbee gave a course of lectures on the industrial revolution
to students reading for Honors in the School of Modern History.
These lectures were extremely well received. In the autumn
of 1882 he offered himself in the North Ward of Oxford as a
Liberal candidate for the Town Council, and made three
speeches chiefly upon those aspects of municipal government
which concern social reform, such as the administration of
poor relief and the construction of artizans' and laborers'
dwellings. He also threw out the idea of volunteer sanitary
committees for the enforcement of the laws relating to public
health. He himself took some steps towards the organization
of such a committee, and many have since been established
elsewhere. In the December of the same year he attended a
Liberal meeting at Newbury, in Berkshire, and made a speech
upon the Land Question and the Agricultural Laborer.

He had for some time been familiar with a book then little
known and since famous—Henry George's " Progress and
Poverty." In this year he wrote in one of his letters to a
sister : " I have known George's book for a very long time.
I always thought it, while full of fallacies and crude conceptions, very remarkable for its style and vigor, and while no
economist would be likely for a moment to be staggered by its
theories, it is very likely to seem convincing to the general
reader. I remember last year at the Master's (*i. e.* Professor
Jowett), Mr. Fawcett asking me to tell him about it—he had
not read it even then." So much was he struck by the book

that he gave two lectures upon it at Oxford in the Michaelmas term of 1882. At the conclusion of the second lecture he made an earnest appeal to his younger hearers not to let the lawful ambitions of life, nor its domestic joys, make them forgetful of the lofty ideals or of the generous resolutions to ameliorate the condition of the poor and neglected which they might have cherished at the University. Many were deeply moved by this appeal, and he afterwards expressed the thought that he might have spoken with too much solemnity, but added, as if by way of excuse, " I could not help it." These lectures were the last which he ever gave in Oxford.

Indeed the end of all things earthly was now very near. For many months past he had been growing pale and haggard. He was wasted almost to a skeleton. His old gaiety had almost forsaken him. The death of his friend and teacher, Professor Green, had deepened his depression. Yet he sought no rest. He faced his growing labors with a stubborn resolution which concealed from his friends and possibly from himself an approaching failure of strength. In the January of 1883, he repeated at St. Andrew's Hall, Newman Street, London, his lectures on "Progress and Poverty." His audience was large and representative. At the first lecture it listened with attention. At the second, a small but noisy minority made a considerable disturbance. His strength had declined in the interval, and from the second lecture he went back to Wimbledon a dying man. In early childhood he had suffered concussion of the brain in consequence of a fall from a pony; and ever since then exhaustion with him was apt to bring on sleeplessness. So worn and excited was he now, that even with the help of the strongest opiates he could get no sleep. His mind, wandering and unstrung, turned again and again to the one preoccupation of his life; to the thought of all the sin and misery in the world. At times a strange unearthly cheerfulness broke through his gloom. He constantly asked to lie in the sun—to let the light stream in upon him; murmuring, "Light purifies—the sun burns up evil—let in the light." He did not experience much bodily suffering; but sleeplessness brought on inflammation of the brain; and after seven weeks of illness he died on the 9th of March, 1883, in the thirty-first year of his age.

He lies beside his father in the churchyard of Wimbledon. It is a beautiful spot, overshadowed with the everlasting verdure of the ilex and cedar. There many generations have found rest from hope and desire; but few or none among them all have been mourned so widely and so sincerely as Arnold Toynbee. It is easy to make a catalogue of the opinions, writings and actions of any man; to enumerate in order the events of his life; to sum up his virtues and his failings: and, this done, we have what they call a life. Yet life is the only thing wanting to such a performance. In every man of fine gifts, there is something, and that the finest element of all, which eludes so rough a procedure. There is something which those who have known him have felt without being able to express; something which pervaded everything he said or did, something unique; irreparable, not to be stated, not to be forgotten. Most indescribable, most exquisite is this charm blending with the freshness of early youth, like the scent of innumerable flowers floating upon a gentle breeze from the ocean. Length of added years would have brought the achievement of tasks hardly begun, the maturity of thoughts freshly conceived, and the just rewards of widely extended fame and reputation; but it could not have added anything to the personal fascination of Arnold Toynbee, or enhanced the sacred regard with which all who had the great happiness to know and the great sorrow to lose him will cherish his memory whilst life endures.

APPENDIX.

LETTER TO THOMAS ILLINGWORTH, Esq., OF BRADFORD.

OXFORD, *January* 21, 1880.

Dear Sir: I have read your very clear account of the credit system as you have seen it in operation with great interest. The facts you give will be of much value as an addition to those usually found in the textbooks on Political Economy. If I understand you rightly, you advocate, as a remedy for the evils we both discern, the adoption of a cash system of trading. But I do not quite see *how* such a system is to be adopted, as long as it is the interest—the immediate interest of firms to give the long credit you speak of in order to obtain custom. That is (as you point out), excessive competition is at the bottom of a reckless credit system, and the problem is, how can we restrain this competition, and make it the *interest* of men to adopt a cash system. Take the analogous case of adulteration. This also is the result of excessive competition. The problem is—How can we make it the *interest* of manufacturers to sell pure goods? It is a well-known fact that honest manufacturers have reluctantly given in to the practice of adulteration because they found that if they refused to execute the orders offered them by merchants, other manufacturers accepted them, and they were driven out of the market. Of course, where a great firm with an established reputation have possession of a market, it may be for their interest to sell unadulterated goods—they may lose their market if their goods deteriorate. But when manufacturers are seeking to make a rapid fortune on borrowed capital, it is often for their interest to sell as much as they can in as short a time as possible. They do not want to build up a trade reputation, but to make money and to leave the trade.

Now I tried to show in my lecture the various restrictions which have made it the *interest* of men to be honest and humane. You cannot expect the great mass of men to be moral unless it is their interest to be moral. That is, if the average man finds that honesty, instead of being the best policy, is the high road to ruin, he will certainly be dishonest, and the whole community suffers. It is obvious that a man will not sell pure milk if he finds that he is being undersold by competitors who sell adulterated

55

milk to careless and ignorant customers—a man will not sell pure goods of any kind if he finds that he is being undersold by those who sell adulterated goods. But why is it possible for the manufacturer to sell adulterated goods? Because of the ignorance, apathy and helplessness of the isolated consumer. If he is not apathetic, he is ignorant and helpless. What does the ordinary consumer know about the quality of goods? Nothing at all.

Now I wished to show that owing to recognized causes consumers *were* forming unions to buy goods—the organization of consumption was taking place. And further I tried to hint the possible effects of this organization of consumption on (1) adulteration, (2) fluctuation of prices due to abuse of the credit system and the factory system. I think the cash system you advocate might be possible, where consumers are organized in unions, because it would there become the *interest* of both buyers and sellers to adopt it.

I agree with you that it is quite possible that retail distribution in the future will take place through enormous stores in the hands of companies or private persons—that there is nothing magical in co-operative stores. But whatever system prevails, there is no doubt that the excessive competition and waste in retail distribution will gradually diminish and that we shall have, instead of innumerable shops, groups of large stores with thousands of permanent customers. That is the first point—*the organization of consumption.* Next it is an admitted fact that the producers and consumers are drawing together owing to the telegraph and improved means of communication. Intermediate agents are being eliminated. One result is that *long* credits are not so necessary as before.

Now in these two points—the organization of consumption and the elimination of the distance between producers and consumers—I think, lies our hope.

(1) For (throwing aside the idea of contracts for terms of years) it will now be possible for the consumer through these stores to buy directly of the producer. The intermediate dealers whose interest it was to "dare forward," etc., are eliminated—the consumer buys, say, at the ordinary trade credit. I need not attempt a more detailed explanation. The only difficulty I see is that different manufacturers in competing for custom might try and outbid each other, offering long credit; but it is more probable that the competition would affect price.

(2) As education and the taste for better goods grows stronger, the consumer will be able through the stores to employ skilful buyers to select unadulterated commodities which he individually could not do. The honest manufacturer would be protected from the competition of dishonest rivals.

(3) Speculation being minimized owing to the elimination of the intermediate agents, it would be possible for manufacturers to anticipate the demand for goods—and this would be facilitated by the concentration of consumers.

But I have said enough. I should like to have drawn out this idea in greater detail, but I am pressed for time. I hope what I have written is intelligible. The question I should like answered is—how would it be possible to procure the adoption of a cash system as things are at present. I do not wish to draw you into a correspondence, but I should like to have an answer on that point. As I said in my last letter, I hope I may some day have the pleasure of talking to you on this subject. I am,

Yours very truly,

ARNOLD TOYNBEE.

P. S.—(1) Is it in the least probable that merchants would associate in order to put an end to the abuse of the credit system? **Is not competition too keen and are not interests** too much at variance?

(2) Legislation on this point would be impossible—would it not?

THE WORK OF TOYNBEE HALL.

By PHILIP LYTTELTON GELL, *Chairman of the Council.*

I have been asked to add to this brief account of Arnold Toynbee an equally brief description of the somewhat complex undertaking now widely known as "Toynbee Hall." Without having been founded by Arnold Toynbee, as is often imagined, without even aiming consciously at the embodiment of his views, nothing could better prove the wide acceptance and stability of those principles of social responsibility upon which Arnold Toynbee in his short life insisted.

Those who have read the preceding pages will have gathered how emphatic an answer Arnold Toynbee gave to the cynical or hopeless appeal of the apostles of *laissez-faire*, "Am I my brother's keeper!" In his own aspirations, in his conversation, in his theories of politics and economics, in the practical activity of his own life, this responsibility was the underlying and undying factor. The results of economical laws were to him not forces to be noted and then accepted, but forces to be wrestled with and controlled by the still superior ascendency of human character. His sense of responsibility made him no Utopian philanthropist, his sense of human injustice and human suffering never made him revolutionary, but only intensified his civic earnestness. He was a good citizen who instinctively seized upon each and every civic institution, seeking to increase its special effectiveness and to ennoble its working for the benefit of his fellow citizens. His views as regards the National Church system and Education, as regards the Poor Law, the Volunteers or the Co-operative movement, the teaching of the Universities or the projects for their Extension in other cities, were all referable to one drift of his character—a natural value for an institution or an organization wherever it had grown up, a far seeing intuition as to the ideal which it ought to serve in the interests of the common weal, and an instinctive tendency to take his own share as a good citizen in its work. I doubt whether this was conscious with him, but it was the same turn of feeling that took him into his lodging in the East End, into workmen's Clubs, or to the Board of Guardians and the Committee of the Charity Organization Society, which enlisted him in the Volunteers, which made him compete for a seat in his Town Council.

This appreciation of the influence and the duties of practical citizenship was far from being limited to Arnold Toynbee. It was at Oxford a time of reaction against the facile theories of the Radicals, of irritation against the cheap philanthropy of "advanced" views ending in no sacrifice of self; of scepticism as to the value of political and social programmes which took no account of the actual complexities of human life and character. At the suggestion of Rev. S. A. Barnett, a liberal London clergyman in an East End parish, who had many friends amongst us, a little University Colony had already been formed in Whitechapel to *do* something for the poor, and when we came to discuss the nature of our memorial to Arnold Toynbee, it was natural with many of us to urge that a "University Settlement in East London" would be the most fitting monument to his memory.

At the time, however, the majority of his friends dwelt rather upon his brief career as an economist, and it was decided to apply the fund placed at our disposal, "The Toynbee Trust," to the investigation of practical points of Political Economy. It was arranged that in each year a young economist should be appointed to spend the winter in some selected industrial centre, giving lectures to the workmen, and simultaneously investigating some important local feature of the industrial organization.[1]

But in that first winter the whole heart of the nation was stirred by the revelations of the *Pall Mall Gazette* as to the lives of the inhabitants of the metropolis, the "Bitter Cry of Outcast London." The facts set forth were neither new nor unknown. They were just those with which the clergy and other workers in East London were most familiar as the daily burden of their lives. But for once they were driven home into the hearts of the well-to-do, and for a space a great deal of emotion was expressed. The newspapers were full of East London. The air was alive with schemes for wild legislation. High officials visited the slums in person. The fashionable world followed in their footsteps. "Sanitary Aid Committees" were formed in every district to enforce upon landlords and parochial officials a stricter observance of the laws which should protect the homes of the poor. For the first time the actual condition of the people flashed upon the generous feelings of the Universities. There were stirring debates at Oxford

---

[1] The subject upon which reports have been thus prepared so far are "Industrial Arbitration in the Northumberland Mining Industries;" "Economic Effects of Mining Royalties;" "Movements of Population amongst Trades."

and Cambridge. For the first time men were startled into a feeling of their responsibility towards the toiling millions whose labors make possible the academic life. Mr. Barnett seized the moment to urge his project of a University Colony in East London, where young men who had been touched with sympathy for the lives of their poorer fellow citizens might live face to face with the actual conditions of crowded city life, study on the spot the evils and their remedies, and if possible ennoble the lives and improve the material condition of the people.

The tinder took fire, and in a burst of general enthusiasm the "Universities Settlement Association" was formed to erect the necessary buildings—Lecture Rooms and Residential Chambers—and to provide funds to support the undertakings of the Residents. The motives of the founders cannot be better stated than in the words of the Appeal which we then issued.

"For some years past the momentous spiritual and social questions involved in the condition of the poor have awakened an increasing interest in our Universities; and the conviction has grown deeper that the problems of the future can only be solved through a more practical experience, and a closer intimacy and sympathy with the poor themselves.

"The main difficulty of poor city neighborhood, where the toilers who create our national prosperity are massed apart, is that they have few friends and helpers who can study and relieve their difficulties, few points of contact with the best thoughts and aspirations of their age, few educated public-spirited residents, such as elsewhere in England uphold the tone of Local Life and enforce the efficiency of Local Self-Government. In the relays of men coming year by year from the Universities into London to study for professions or to pursue their independent interests, there are many, free from the ties of later life, who might fitly choose themselves to live amongst the poor, to give up to them a portion of their lives, and endeavor to fill this social void. The universal testimony of those best acquainted with the squalor and degradation to which attention has been lately directed, affirms that there is less need of new legislation than of citizens who will maintain the existing law and create a public opinion amongst the poor themselves. Upon the Vestries, upon the Boards of Guardians, upon the Committees of Schools and of every public undertaking, educated men may find the opportunity of serving the interests of their neighbors: or even if such direct responsibilities cannot be assumed, they may help to create amongst their fellow-citizens the public opinion which insists on good administration. University men have already approached the Higher Education of the working classes in the University Extension Scheme and institutions with similar aims. The results have been most encouraging. The time has come for a far wider development. Art and Industrial Exhibitions have to be organized at the doors of the poor, and, what is more important, explained sympathetically to the throngs ready to visit them. Co-operative Societies have to be formed,

their principles established, and their wider **issues** developed.   Other
helpers are wanted for the work of the Charity Organization and Sanitary
Aid Committees, for the organization of Clubs, Excursions, Childrens'
Country Holidays, Concerts, and for every kind of Entertainment in which
the culture born of ease may be shared with the **toiling** population.

"It is the object of the 'Universities' **Settlement'** **to** link the Universities with East London, and to direct the human sympathies, the energies, and the public spirit of Oxford and Cambridge to the actual conditions
of town life.   During the last few years many University men, following in
the steps of Denison and Arnold Toynbee, have, on leaving the Universities for London, energetically responded to the varied calls for their aid.
Such isolated efforts are capable of infinite expansion were the way once
laid open, and it is now proposed to offer to those who are ready a channel
of immediate and useful activity and a centre of right living.   In a common
life united by a common devotion to the welfare of the poor, those fellow-
workers **who** are able to give either their whole time or the leisure which
they **can** spare from their occupations, will find, it is believed, a support in
the pursuit **of** their own highest aims as well **as a** practical guidance which
isolated **and** inexperienced philanthropists **must** lack."

The residents (who live at their own charges)[1] **have, by this time, under**
the general direction of Mr. Barnett, turned **into fact** many of the projects
thus set before them.   Upwards of 50 men **have made their home for a**
time at Toynbee Hall, many having now gone **on to their life work,** richer
in social experience and wider in human sympathy.   **The places of** those
who have left have been filled again and again, **and the Chambers are**
generally occupied.   Around the Residents a body **of about 100 "Associ-
ates"** have gathered whose homes lie elsewhere, but **who** co-operate with
the residents in their undertakings, while the Guest rooms have afforded
a temporary hospitality to constant relays of friends, Graduates and Undergraduates, who come to help or to learn for a few days at a time.   Indeed
the "Settlement" tends more and more to become a house of call for earnest
men of all classes, drawn thither by their work, their enquiries, their friendships, **or** invited for the particular discussion of some social problem.

One **object** at least of the founders of the Association has been thus
attained **in** the intercourse established between the life of our Universities
and the life of our East End citizens.   Meanwhile Toynbee Hall has
already succeeded in making its influence widely felt among the crowded
population in whose midst it is placed.   By the **working** classes of East
London it is rapidly being accepted as the **visible embodiment of** the
almost legendary life and culture of the old **Universities.**

It would take too long **to** enumerate in **detail all the** educational and

[1] The Rentals paid by them vary according to accommodation.   They average about £1
weekly.   The arrangements for Board and Service are managed by a Committee of the
Residents and amount to about 25 shillings a week more.

social work in which the residents are engaged. They themselves possibly would feel they had won success in the degree to which they had kindled local opinion and enlisted in every kind of public undertaking the independent co-operation of their neighbors. The residents would judge themselves not so much by what they do, as by what they establish; not by the results which they could report, as by the spirit they have engendered. It is not, we believe, through external interference, but through the development of individual character, through the kindling of local opinion, through the education of civic spirit, and the direction of local energies, that ground can be permanently gained. In a democratic country nothing can be firmly achieved except through the masses of the people. Legislation may strike off the shackles of evil custom, and may supply methods of action, but when the people is enthroned, it is impossible to establish permanently a higher political life, or a more perfect social organization than the people crave for. Every social question has thus a moral question behind. Apathy, isolation, ignorance, selfishness in the masses—these are the powers of resistance to be vanquished before, by any chance, a self-governed people can possibly come to be a well-governed people.

It is not therefore so much by what they have done that the residents would count their days, as by what they may have led others to do. Has any one, coming to Toynbee Hall whether as boy or man, as a student, as a guest, or as a coadjutor in some social undertaking, gained an idea or a method, a belief, a sympathy or a principle which will take its own root in him and bring forth fruit for others' service? Has any one coming from East London or West become inspired with a higher sense of personal and civic duty, with a fuller faith of what can be attained by the fellow-service of fellow-citizens, and by an insight into the possibilities and the methods of social co-operation? Above all, has any one coming to Toynbee Hall, whether rich or poor, found there new sympathies, interests, and friendships, and left it with his old sense of class distinctions, class prejudices, and class antagonisms effaced, in a deeper conviction of human brotherhood and in the acknowledgment of a common responsibility for the common good?

Such at least would be our hope. How far realized we cannot judge. We can only indicate a few of the tangible undertakings which have begun to take root at Toynbee Hall.

Not only has the Hall become the centre of educational effort and social life in Whitechapel, but its members have gone out to take their share in the local government of the district and in all the various forms of public work, to which the manifold needs of a poor, populous, and neglected neighborhood give occasion.

The public rooms of the Hall have become an arena for the discussion of every kind of view, and a meeting place for every class. They have also been made a social centre for every branch of East End life and work, where our hospitalities have been extended to co-operators, workmen's clubs of all kinds, students of every degree, elementary teachers and the representatives of every social movement amongst the people around.   It is no exaggeration to say that many thousands of our poorer fellow-citizens, to whom Toynbee Hall was dedicated by the Universities four years ago, have found recreation and benefit in the rooms established for their use and entertainment.

On the educational side Toynbee Hall has been made the most prominent centre of "University Extension" in East London.   A free students' library has been built and filled with books and readers, lectures and reading clubs ranging over the most varied subjects of moral, literary and scientific interest have been instituted.   Technical classes have been established, musical societies have been formed, and above all the elementary schoolmasters and pupil teachers of the neighborhood, upon whom depends the future of the rising generation of citizens, have been welcomed to the society and the educational advantages of the Hall.

The educational associations which have gathered around us, besides promoting knowledge and developing intellectual interest, have created a spirit of comradeship among the students, inspiring them with a healthy sense of being fellow laborers in a great cause.   Some of the most zealous local students, who are already more or less at home in Toynbee Hall, have taken up residence under academic discipline in "Wadham House," an adjacent building provided for the purpose by residents and their friends. Earning their living during the day, in the evening they pursue their studies in connection with our varied educational classes, and also take their part in its social work.   The home thus offered to men who have to make their own fight for each step in self-improvement, introduces into the heart of East London the elements of an intellectual society, and it promises to form an independent centre of energetic practical citizenship.

It may afford some insight into the magnitude and variety of the claims made upon the time and energy of the inmates of Toynbee Hall, to give a summary of the work done by one of their number, though most of them have their own employments which limit their energies within bounds somewhat more circumscribed.   Besides conducting a class of University Extension Students in popular Ethics, another of Pupil-teachers in English Literature, a class of workingmen in Political Economy, and a Sunday Bible Class of members of the St. Jude's Juvenile Association, the resident in question acted as Secretary to one of the Local Committees of the Charity Organization Society, as Secretary to a Ward Sanitary Aid Committee, as a School Board Manager, and finally as a member of the Board of Guardians.   In each of these capacities he found new fields of work opening out before him.   The Political Economy Class served as the nucleus of a body of workmen, who, as members of relief committees and as managers of the newly-started Recreative Evening Classes in Board Schools, have begun to do excellent service in charitable and educational administration, and have thus given practical evidence of the possibility of developing among the artisans of East London that spirit of citizenship—a very different thing

from political partizanship—which it should be the object of all true reformers to call into existence among the body of the people. In addition **to** these numerous undertakings, in all of which his efforts have been directed to evoking the co-operation of the people themselves, the resident **in** question has found time to devote many evenings to a boys' club, where boxing and single-stick have been substituted for mere horse-play with excellent effect upon the conduct and bearing of the lads. He has also taken a part in organizing foot-ball among the Board Schools of the district.

Records of similar, though in each case individual and distinctive, activity might be given with **respect** to other residents, **but** it is only possible to notice some of the principal results. The "Whittington," a club and home for street boys, was opened in 1885 by Prince Edward of Wales. **It has** done much useful work, **and a** cadet corps of Volunteers has been **formed** there. An effort has been **made to** unite the boy pupil-teachers of all **the** London Elementary Schools **into one** community, and by the agencies **of** cricket, rowing, and debating clubs, **to** kindle amongst them that *esprit de corps* which so strengthens the *morale* of our higher public schools. Numer- **ous classes for** pupil-teachers are conducted by members of **the** Hall, in **all of which the** object kept in view is not so much to increase **the** information **of** the already over-crammed, as to quicken their intellectual interest and widen their sympathies.

The Sanitary Aid Committee, which has its head-quarters at Toynbee Hall, has resulted not only in the removal of a number of specific nuisances, but in greater vigilance both on the part of the landlords and of the **local** authorities with regard to the condition of tenement houses. The **oppor-** tunity which the visitors gain **of** becoming acquainted with the **lives of the** people and of **entering into** friendly relations with them is a **secondary but valuable result.**

Such are some of the undertakings which now centre round Toynbee Hall. **It is an** enterprise which **if** patiently and loyally maintained and effectively **developed cannot** but beget experience which **will** react most practically upon the thought of the educated classes **on whom** in a demo- cratic country falls so **deep a** responsibility for local and **central** good gov- ernment. The present residents at Toynbee Hall are we hope the pioneers of a permanent movement re-establishing amongst **the** leisured classes the **sense of** their civic obligations. **In the** meetings **which** are held in **the** various Colleges in support of the work, the interest of the undergraduates **is** attracted **to** the social questions which confront their representatives **in** Whitechapel, and seed is sown which will bear fruit in years to come, **when the** undergraduates of to-day become the administrators, the landlords, **the journalists, the law** makers, the public opinion of **their** time. **Later as these** undergraduates leave the university, Toynbee **Hall** offers to all an opportunity of direct personal experience of social **problems,** and a channel for the expression of every social sympathy. These are **among** the advan- tages with which **the movement** has endowed the **Universities.** Yet on the

other side we are glad to realize how much tangible good our fellow citizens
have reaped in education, in enlightenment, in social stimulus, in the
development of local life and the reform of local evils.   The principle of
personal service, personal knowledge and personal sympathy remains the
key-note of every endeavor.   On each side men have learnt to appreciate
each other better, and many a link of cordial and deep-rooted friendship,
based on common tastes, common associations and common work for others'
good, now binds together classes which had otherwise been strangers, and
possibly antagonists.

PHILIP LYTTELTON GELL, M. A.,
Chairman of the Council.
***Clarendon** Press and Balliol College, Oxford.*

THE NEIGHBORHOOD GUILD IN NEW YORK.

By Charles B. Stover, A. B.

An apology for appending to the foregoing narrative of the splendid achievements of Toynbee Hall an account of the small doings of the Neighborhood Guild is supplied first, by the fact, that in some measure the descent of the Neighborhood Guild is traceable to Toynbee Hall, and secondly, by the endeavors of the Guild to become the Toynbee Hall of New York City.

The Neighborhood Guild was founded by Mr. Stanton Coit early in 1887, at 146 Forsyth St., New York. After a residence of several weeks among the tenement-house people, face to face with the great problems presented by their lives, Mr. Coit began his work of reform in a tentative manner, by inviting to his own cheerful apartments a club of half a dozen boys, who had been meeting in the dismal room of a poor old blind woman. These boys brought in others, and soon Mr. Coit felt encouraged to rent the basement of the tenement, in which he lived, for a club-room. Here the boys, or young men, their average age being eighteen years, were organized into a club. And afterwards, as the necessary volunteer workers were secured, three other clubs were formed, one consisting of young women, another of little boys, and the last, of little girls. A kindergarten also was established at an early date. These various organized bodies of young people together form the Neighborhood Guild. Its motto is: *"Order is our Basis; Improvement our Aim; and Friendship our Principle."*

In the second year of the Guild's history, the formation of a similar set of clubs was undertaken in Cherry St., and now is being carried on with such ease that our castles in the air become less insubstantial, and our hope grows firmer that the Guild may multiply its clubs on all sides, until, let us say, they shall be found in every election-district of our city ward. Then, when the whole people shall be organized for reform, when all the latent love of the beautiful and the right which the coarseness of tenement-house life and the cares of poverty blast and make unfruitful, shall be stirred up and developed by extensive coöperation for individual and social progress, then shall the workers for righteousness strive to some purpose. But now the workers of iniquity flourish. The poor people of our district are represented in the State Assembly by one of the most notorious scamps in the history of New York politics,—a saloon-keeper, a gambler, a friend of "crooks" and a tool of lobbyists. Four times in succession this law-breaker has been elected a law-maker of the State of New York. "He knows every man, woman, and child in the ward." There is the secret of his power. So says one of his "heelers." Verily the children of this world are wiser in their methods of work than the children of light.

Thus to organize the young people into numerous clubs is to take advantage of their social instinct which, in our tenement-house district, is already finding its gratification in countless "Pleasure Clubs," the height of whose ambition is a chowder-party in summer and a ball in winter. These Pleasure Clubs encourage lavish expenditure of small earnings, vulgarize the tastes, and readily become centres of political jobbery. The Neighborhood Guild Clubs are designed to encourage thrift and fellow-helpfulness, to purify and exalt the tastes, to excite opposition to all forms of injustice, and to kindle devotion to the common weal.

I shall write but briefly of the Guild's forms of entertainment and education, which for the most part are those employed at Toynbee Hall and in the "Annexes" of modern churches; and then more fully of the Guild as a College or University Settlement. Each club meets twice a week. In the older clubs one-fourth of the income from the weekly fee of ten cents is spent for the relief of the sick and the poor. It is our endeavor also to have the clubs bear a portion of the expense of practical reforms. They bore one-third of the expense of keeping our street clean during the summer. The Kindergarten, in charge of two well-trained teachers, gleams like a fairy-land amid the gloomy and depressing tenements. Of the fifty children in attendance at the close of last session, but three are in this year's class. This may be largely ascribed to the removal of families, which among the poor of the city so often interrupts good influences. The untamed small boys, though long subjected to our strongest subduing forces, are still sadly prone to remind us, that for them, to be noisy is to be happy. They tire of every game but base-ball. The piano and song are great aids to composing their wild spirits. The chief instruction given the two girls' clubs is in housewifely duties. The larger girls have been carefully trained in handsewing, including the art of fine embroidery. Several times they have coöperated with the young men's club in getting up musical, literary, and theatrical entertainments. The young men have received the most varied instruction, embracing clay-modelling, wood-carving, debating, public declamation, parliamentary practice, singing, drawing, gymnastic and military drilling. Numerous desultory lectures have been delivered. At present a somewhat systematic effort is being made to give them a grasp of the leading phases of the world's history. Several classes in elementary studies have been formed.

Our "Dancing Evening," for a while weekly, then, as our more serious work increased, semi-monthly, is to be reckoned among the educational, as well as among the entertaining, meetings of the Guild. Only an ignorant fanatic could say that by permitting the young men and the young women to dance together, we are training them for the Bowery dance-halls. People of common sense, with no slight disapproval of dancing, have come here and for a long while observed its effects upon these young people, and **now** unhesitatingly declare that these social meetings, always under the supervision of some of the Guild's workers, have proved a school of graceful, modest, **and** chivalrous manners, all the corrupting influences of dance-hall and fashionable ball to the contrary notwithstanding.

In the summer-time, to a limited extent the clubs **leave** the city for a breath of fresh air. The little girls, in several parties, spent a week at the country home of their teacher. Very generous invitations were extended to the young women's club to spend a week or more at the sea-shore, and to the young men's club to summer in the Catskills; but not one of the young men could leave the city, **and** only three of the young women could go away, chiefly because their employers would not grant them leave **of absence**. Several excursions of a day have been made by two or **more of the clubs to** the shores **of Staten Island,** where bathing, boating, and **athletic sports** afforded grateful recreation.

The work of the Guild, as thus outlined, is carried on in the main by **volunteer workers, who** in this second year of the Guild's history numbered **twenty-two, one-half** ladies and one-half gentlemen. Of these workers the great majority are up-town residents, who come to the Guild an evening or **two every week.** They bring with them gentleness, kindness, culture, knowledge, a rich store of human sympathy, and open eyes to discern **the signs of** the times. These are some of the strands which help to bridge over **that** angry flood of passions **which** is ever tending to sweep the social classes farther apart. The Guild **is** not tainted with fashionable "slumming." A little of its work has been done up town. One lady in her own home instructed a young man **in** piano-playing and singing; another in **her** own home instructed a **girl** in embroidering; and still another gave lessons **in wood-carving to three young men.** Would there were more such intercourse between up-town people and tenement-house people! The Guild aims **to be a mediator between the** cultured and the uncultured, between the gifted and **the ungifted.** Ye that have talents, why not impart to him that has **none?** What a university might be established in this city, its curriculum perhaps **not** as varied as that of a regular university, but possessing an unrivalled endowment of saving social forces, if a thousand young men and women from the tenement-houses were welcomed weekly into as many different homes of the up-town people, there to receive some acquirement from more gifted fellow-creatures!

The Guild's most distinctive feature is found in its College men, resident together in a tenement-house. Of these there have been five,—Mr. Stanton Coit, Ph. D. (Berlin Univ.), Mr. E. S. Forbes, and Mr. W. B. Thorp, all Amherst graduates; Mr. M. I. Swift, Ph. D. (Johns Hopkins University), a Williams graduate, and the writer, a Lafayette graduate. Three of these men have been students at the University of Berlin. Mr. Coit, during his student life abroad, became well acquainted with Toynbee Hall, where he was enriched with new ideas and impulses. However, his prime endeavor here seems to have been not to model the Guild after Toynbee Hall, viewed as a University Settlement, but rather, in accordance with his own ethical system, so **to** organize the people around the *family*, **as** the unit, as to originate forces of social regeneration. **This organization has** not extended to the parents. In describing his work among the young, Mr. Coit has said that he resolved to do for them, what parents of wealth and leisure would do for their children. Also another Guild resident **came** in contact with Toynbee Hall while abroad, and, at the first moment of **his** acquaintance with the Guild, became attached to it by the expectation of its becoming another Toynbee Hall. I well remember when in May, **1887**, I **asked** Mr. Coit whether such might not be the development of the Guild, **he** replied, "Will you help to make it a Toynbee Hall." He made special trips to Amherst and Johns Hopkins to enlist men in the movement. **Mr.** Swift, for whom the idea of a People's University had great attractions, helped along the Toynbee Hall movement here by his successful management of a Social Science Club, in which, to a limited extent, workingmen were brought in contact with University men.

Let us notice some of the reasons for developing the Neighborhood Guild into a Toynbee Hall. First. There is a numerous class of educated young men, who are deeply interested in the social problems of to-day, their sympathies for human suffering the warmest, who yet **would be** hampered, if **put** in ecclesiastical leading-strings. Such would **find a field** of **labor in a** Toynbee Hall. Let it not be thought, that I **presume to speak to the dis**credit of the Church. I am regarding her conservatism in **methods of work** simply as a matter of fact, which exercises a decided influence over **the** career of many a young man. I know that one, inspired by the love of **Christ** and his fellowmen, applied for work to a person in authority in city evangelization, and was dismissed with the rash words: "The Lord God has no work for you to do;" because, forsooth, his theology seemed "wishy-washy" to the rigid dogmatist. Such a young man is welcome here. Not because the Guild has a liking for vague theology, but because it believes that this world is too badly off to afford to let a single spark of enthusiasm **for** humanity be quenched.

Further, a Toynbee Hall could easily approach the workingman, **who** is now estranged from the Church. Ex-Pres. McCosh has lately said that **when he first** visited our country, he was often asked, "What do you think of our congregations?" and he answered, "I think much of them, but where are your laboring classes?" and he adds, "Where is the laboring man in our Churches? is the question I am still putting, seeking an answer." It should also be noticed that the Church is much estranged from the tenement-house districts. As the Church is doing very little for the down-town people, a University Settlement would here find a large field of labor. These people should not be utterly forsaken. According to the New York "City Mission Monthly," in our ward, the 10th, the population is 47,554, and the number of churches and chapels, five. And according to Dr. Josiah Strong, while the increase in the population of New York City, since 1880, was 300,000, the increase in the number of churches, during the same period, was only four. I do not wish to imply that a Toynbee Hall would be a complete substitute for the vanished churches; but would anyone deter another from pouring balm upon a cut finger, because there is no surgeon at hand to remove some internal cancer? So I believe in this University movement, because it *does* benefit men. How far it falls short of blessing and regenerating the entire man does not enter into consideration now. This is the Guild's relation to the Christian Church. Never, not even when Mr. Coit was here, was the Guild antagonistic to the Church. I say, not even when Mr. Coit was here; for his late position, as Assistant Lecturer to the New York Society for Ethical Culture, seems to have created, in some minds, the impression that this Guild is a work of that Society, and that the spirit of Ethical Culture, with its pronounced repudiation of all theology, rules in the Guild. These notions are utterly false. The personal help of Christians in the Clubs was always welcomed by Mr. Coit; and we have even been scrupulous enough to hold all our meetings on week-days, that on Sunday no member of the Clubs might be withdrawn from attendance on Sunday School or Church.

Further, various educational, sanitary, social, and political reforms could be undertaken by a Toynbee Hall with fewer restraints than they could by the Church. Certainly in political action it could engage with a freedom to which the Church is a stranger. From a Toynbee Hall might proceed a thorough purification of this sink of political corruption. Persons resident here would acquire that familiarity with the men and the affairs of the district which is so necessary for a successful reform movement. Our local "boss" says: "We will not allow the residents of Murray Hill to dictate to us." May the time come when a large band of intelligent, fearless, and public-spirited young men, residents here, shall labor perseveringly for the purity of the ballot and the dethronement of the corrupt "bosses!"

Something may be said also in favor of such a University Settlement from a purely intellectual point of view. That the University-bred mind would itself be profited by frequent contact with the masses of a great city no one doubts. But very generally it is supposed that the University-bred mind is altogether unsuited to instruct and inspire the masses. I remember that once in a Social Science Club, made up, according to the Club's parlance, of *proletaires* and professors, a University man, having alluded to the difficulty, which a person like himself has in reaching the understanding of the people, a workingman remarked,—"I once heard Huxley lecture and had no difficulty in understanding him." Does the multitude have any difficulty in understanding the political addresses of our leading lawyers and statesmen? Is the popular mind capable of grasping only the platitudes of pettifoggers? Why is it that in New York City the ablest and most attractive preachers are in the pulpits of the rich? If Christ and St. Paul were here, would they confine their preaching to wealthy churches, and think the poor of the tenements quite incapable of appreciating their sermons? **I** dare say that the most powerful and popular of the preachers to **men of** wealth and culture could, with little effort, render themselves both powerful and popular in the slums. Let not the University men be misled by the foibles of the Church. A great work can be done by them right in the heart of the tenements. That the intellectual barriers to their **success** can be overcome, the story of Toynbee Hall amply testifies.

May this monograph concerning Arnold Toynbee and the accompanying sketch of the work of Toynbee Hall incite many an American student to a similar work in his own land!